At The
FOOT
Of The
CROSS

At The Foot Of The Cross

A CALL TO RETURN
TO THE CROSS OF CHRIST

At The
FOOT
Of The
CROSS

IMO-ABASI JACOB, SNR

At The Foot Of The Cross

REHOBOTH HOUSE™

At The Foot Of The Cross
A Call To Return To The Cross Of Christ

Copyright © 2018 By Imo-Abasi Jacob, Snr

This book is published in the United States of America by Rehoboth House, Chicago and printed by permission in Nigeria by Rehoboth Publishing, Lagos.

Unless otherwise identified, scripture quotations are from the King James Version of the Bible. All emphasis within the scripture quotes are the author's own.

Forward Enquiries to Imo-Abasi Jacob, Snr for teachings, seminars and workshops on the Cross and any of his other books:
imoabasi@yahoo.com or call 234-1-8027782240

Placing Online Orders for the Book
Amazon.com or via HYPERLINK "mailto:*imoabasi@yahoo.com*" *imoabasi@yahoo.com*

Haggai Business School Email: HYPERLINK "mailto:*haggaischool@yahoo.co.uk*" *haggaischool@yahoo.co.uk*

Interior and Cover Designed by Rehoboth House, Chicago
www.rehobothhouseonline.com
email:info@rehobothhouseonline.com

First Print, March 2018
Printed in the Federal Republic of Nigeria by Permission
By Rehoboth Publishing, 174 Ikorodu Road, Lagos.
Tel: 234-802-304-3072
E-mail: rehobothpublishing@gmail.com

At The Foot Of The Cross

Table Of Contents

Dedication

This book is dedicated to the Ministers and Members of Chosen Vessels Assembly (CVA), Uyo, Nigeria, who have used my teachings on the Cross for their Easter Programme since 2014.

At The Foot Of The Cross

Acknowledgements

This book is borne out of the teachings at Easter Programmes of Chosen Vessels Assembly in Uyo, Akwa Ibom State, Nigeria. My appreciation goes to Pastor Patrick Edet, who after reading my book, The Three Silent Days and Nights, invited me to conduct an Easter Teaching Programme on the Power of the Cross in 2014 and subsequently use my teaching on the Cross at every Easter to date. Each chapter of this book, At the Foot of the Cross, is the theme used for the successive years since 2014. I also want to thank Pastor Unwana Bassey, Pastor Sampson and the Chosen Vessels Assembly Choir for the backup during the teaching on the Cross. Pastor Unwana Bassey, specifically, encouraged me to convert the teachings into a book, and I am grateful for his prompting. I thank Mr. Aniekan Abraham for writing the Foreword to the book and offering his insights on the Cross.

I thank my wife, Mrs. Rosemary Imo-Abasi Jacob and my children for allowing me the time to prepare and conduct the teaching programme at Chosen Vessels Assembly.

Most of all, I thank the LORD Jesus Christ for the revelation on the Cross and the favour over the years culminating in the publication of this book.

Foreword

The Cross of Jesus Christ is the focal point and the fulcrum of Christian faith. Without the Cross of Jesus Christ, Christianity will be like any other religion. It is the Cross that makes the difference in Christianity. The Cross of Christ epitomizes the boundless love of God for mankind. It was on the Cross that the supreme price for our redemption was paid fully Jesus Christ, the Son of the Living God. The Cross of Jesus Christ reminds us of the total defeat of the devil and his cohorts and our freedom from the devil's captivity.

This book, At the Foot of the Cross is a profound exposition of the revelations of the finished work of atonement that Jesus Christ accomplished on the Cross at Calvary for mankind. It is sad however, to observe that today, the Church has unwittingly taken a detour from the teachings of the Cross to its own destruction. It's no wonder that today, the Church has become weak and powerless. The teaching of the Cross is far disappearing from many pulpits today. The reigning messages are on prosperity, greatness and the like.

At the Foot of the Cross, is a wake-up call to the Church to make a U-turn and return to the teachings of the Cross of Jesus Christ. The author has brilliantly elucidated on the different thematic aspects of the revelations of the Cross of Jesus Christ to humanity. In discussing each of these themes which he developed into chapters, he used relevant Scriptures copiously to support them.

The last chapter of this book, "The Ultimate Decision" reminds the reader that life is a bundle of choices. The choice we make today, may carry eternal consequences. One of the choices we must make in life is the choice to accept Jesus Christ as one's personal Lord and Saviour and to walk with Him. I join the author to implore you to make that decision today, to follow Jesus Christ. Delay is dangerous and tomorrow may be too late. This book is simply a must read treaty; I recommend it to all believers and non-believers. Happy reading and God bless you.

Pastor Aniekan Abraham
Pastor, Four Square Church
Uyo, Nigeria.

Preface

The teaching on the Cross of Christ has become a lost coin in contemporary Christian expositions. Teaching on the Cross is overshadowed by populist topics such as prosperity, deliverance and person and group motivation. And unless something is done and done quick, today's Christianity may drift from its foundation: the cross of Christ. My book, The Three Silent Days and Nights, was a lamentation on all that was wrong with a Christianity without the Cross. The book invited readers to examine the events of the three days leading to the Cross, during the burial and resurrection of our Lord and Saviour, Jesus Christ, in a way that challenged conventional beliefs over the observances of Easter, Lent, Christmas, etc.

This book, At the Foot of the Cross, starts where the book, The Three Silent Days and Nights, ends. This book is an attempt to invite the Church not only to the Cross but to require the Church to weave everything around the Cross, whether doctrines or practices or hope or the eternal redemption of man. We believe that the Cross was not a snapshot of a historic event but an eternal plan, promoted from eternity past and actualised for eternity present and eternity future. That is why this book ends with a chapter, The Eternal Cross.

The focus of this book is to examine and learn from the responses by the first audience at the foot of the Cross, including the religious establishment (the Jewish priesthood), the political establishment (the Roman Government), the Disciples, the Women, the Centurion (Soldiers), the thieves on the Cross, and onlookers. Though these were eyewitnesses to the event at Calvary where Jesus was crucified, they all misunderstood the Cross until the post-resurrection expositions by the Lord Jesus Christ, the Holy Spirit, and the early Apostles who set in order the truth of the Cross of Christ in relation to the Christian faith. The conversation the LORD had with two of the disciples on the road to Emmaus revealed the disconnect, even by the eyewitnesses of the cross, to scriptures and prophecies that heralded the Cross.

> *"Then he said unto them, O fools, and slow of heart to believe all that the prophets have spoken: Ought not Christ to have suffered these things, and to enter into his glory? And beginning at Moses and all the prophets, he expounded unto them in all the scriptures the things concerning himself" Luke 24:25-27.*

The preaching of the Cross still elicits different responses from different people up till now. Paul understood this problem and drew the attention of the Corinthian believers to the central theme of the Cross. He concluded that in the weakness of the Cross, the power of God had been made manifest.

> *"For the preaching of the cross is to them that perish foolishness; but unto us which are saved it is the power of God"* *1 Corinthians 1:18.*

Paul presented a deeper insight to the Cross throughout all his epistles and was persuaded to sum his life goal around the Cross in these words:

> *"For I determined not to know anything among you, save Jesus Christ, and him crucified" 1 Corinthians 2:2.*

Indeed, the Cross is so central to the Christian faith that a detour from it makes Christianity impotent. This book, therefore, is a call for the Church to return to the Cross, embrace it, preach it, make it her central focus and live by it. The book is an exposition of the victory of the Cross, the glory of the Cross, the sufficiency of the Cross, counting the cost of the Cross, the offenses of the Cross and the eternal Cross. We will explore these themes and many more as we delve into the book.

Imo-Abasi Jacob, Snr

March 1, 2018

CHAPTER ONE

A Call To The Cross Of Christ

Hymn: When I Survey the Wondrous Cross
1.When I survey the wondrous cross
On which the Prince of glory died,
My richest gain I count but loss,
And pour contempt on all my pride.

2. Forbid it, Lord, that I should boast,
Save in the death of Christ my God!
All the vain things that charm me most,
I sacrifice them to His blood.

3. See from His head, His hands, His feet,
Sorrow and love flow mingled down!
Did e'er such love and sorrow meet,
Or thorns compose so rich a crown?

4. Were the whole realm of nature mine,
That were a present far too small;
Love so amazing, so divine,
Demands my soul, my life, my all.

The Hymn, "When I survey the Wondrous Cross", is a gentle reminder of the need to constantly explore the Cross, its meaning, ramifications and our commitment to it. If we lose sight of the Cross, nothing is left of Christianity. Our response to the appeal of the Cross reveals our commitment to the cause of Christ here on earth. Over the ages, men who have come to the Cross have revealed their commitment to or the lack of it to the cause of Christ.

We examine here two ways men have responded to the Cross of Christ from the time of the crucifixion to the time when the epistles were written. These reveal interesting perspectives to learn from and make a strong case for believers to return to the truth of the Cross. The Cross attracts but it is in the response of those who have come to it that matters. Over the ages, we see two scenes at the Cross, as follows:

Scene#1: Eye Witnessing Of The Cross

There were many people at the foot of the Cross when Jesus was crucified. They had different impressions about the Cross. Some wondered what it all meant, some made positive conclusions, some mocked while others held their breath and comments. We have classified 11 sets of eye witnesses of the Cross, as follows:

Certain women, including Mary, the mother of Jesus, and John (the Beloved Disciple) drew near to the Cross and stood by to observe all that went on. The LORD conversed with them despite His agony and their bewilderment. This group of eye witnesses represents those who had genuine interest in the events of the Cross. They drew near to the foot of the Cross in spite of the risk of persecution by the Chief Priests and prosecution by the Roman Authority.

> "Now there stood by the cross of Jesus his mother, and his mother's sister, Mary the wife of Cleophas, and Mary Magdalene. When Jesus therefore saw his mother, and the disciple standing by, whom he loved, he saith unto his mother, Woman, behold thy son! Then saith he to the disciple, Behold thy mother! And from that hour that disciple took her unto his own home" John 19:25-27.

One other eye witness was Simon of Cyrene who was compelled by the Roman soldiers to carry the Cross on the way to Golgatha. Simon was on his way out of the City when this fate fell on him. This eye witness played a unique role at the foot of the Cross. Though he was compelled, he took the burden of the Cross upon his hands and shoulders and trekked the rough road uphill to Calvary. He must have sweated as he trekked, wondering why he was so maltreated, him being a foreigner. There is no record of what he said. All the gospel accounts agree that he was compelled.

"And as they came out, they found a man of Cyrene, Simon by name: him they compelled to bear his cross" Matthew 27:32.

Luke and John accounts of the incidence suggest that Simon assisted the LORD to bear the Cross as both bore the Cross. Luke's account had it that "… they laid hold upon one Simon, a Cyrenian, coming out of the country, and on him they laid the cross, that he might bear it after Jesus" (Luke 23:26). He bore the Cross after Jesus. He took over from Jesus. John's accounted that "And he bearing his cross went forth into a place called the place of a skull, which is called in the Hebrew Golgotha: (John 19:17). This confirms that Jesus also bore the Cross, probably at the start of the journey to Golgatha before Simon came in (as recorded in the Synoptic Gospels) to complete the journey with the Cross to Golgatha.

Another eye witness was the Centurion, a Roman army officer, who was probably in charge of the crucifixion or mounting of guard at the scene. When the Centurion and his band of soldiers saw the natural occurrences (earth quake) following the crucifixion, they made a positive confession about the Cross of Christ.

"Now when the centurion, and they that were with him, watching Jesus, saw the earthquake, and those things that were done, they feared greatly, saying, Truly this was the Son of God" Matthew 27:54.

Luke's account of the Centurion's response is that when he saw what was done, he glorified God and made a positive confession about Jesus.

> *"Now when the centurion saw what was done, he glorified God, saying, Certainly this was a righteous man" Luke 23:47.*

"There were other eye witnesses whom the Bible simply describes as passers-by who reviled the LORD, wagged their heads and cast aspersion about the Cross. They missed the point even from the vantage position of witnessing an important event that would determine their eternal destiny.

> *And they that passed by reviled him, wagging their heads, And saying, Thou that destroyest the temple, and buildest it in three days, save thyself. If thou be the Son of God, come down from the cross" Matthew 27:39-40.*

The Chief Priests, the Scribes and the Elders (the religious establishment), who superintended over the crucifixion of the LORD, mocked Him and missed the point on the efficacy of the Cross.

> *"Likewise also the chief priests mocking him, with the scribes and elders, said, He saved others; himself he cannot save. If he be the King of Israel, let him now come*

down from the cross, and we will believe him. He trusted in God; let him deliver him now, if he will have him: for he said, I am the Son of God" Matthew 27:41-43.

Another set of eye witnesses was the two thieves on their cross. These two were privileged to experience crucifixion at the same time with the LORD. They had a direct conversation with the LORD and yet one of them missed the import of the Cross and went to perdition. The other made a positive confession of the Cross and shared a place in eternity with the LORD.

"And one of the malefactors which were hanged railed on him, saying, If thou be Christ, save thyself and us. But the other answering rebuked him, saying, Dost not thou fear God, seeing thou art in the same condemnation? And we indeed justly; for we receive the due reward of our deeds: but this man hath done nothing amiss. And he said unto Jesus, Lord, remember me when thou comest into thy kingdom. And Jesus said unto him, Verily I say unto thee, Today shalt thou be with me in paradise" Luke 23:39-43.

There were those who were speechless and who stood gazing at the Cross. They were overwhelmed by the tragedy of the Cross and perplexed at what the future held for them. There was nothing like it before and so words were not enough to capture their perplexity. We can simply conclude that they were speechless.

"And all the people that came together to that sight, beholding the things which were done, smote their breasts, and returned. And all his acquaintance, and the women that followed him from Galilee, stood afar off, beholding these things" Luke 23:48-49.

There were those who could not stand the risk of the Cross and so they fled for safety and some relocated from Jerusalem. Unfortunately, included in this group were the disciples of Jesus Christ. Even though the LORD had told them beforehand the events of the Cross, they were so discouraged by the risk of facing persecution and prosecution that they had to hide for safety or fled.

"But all this was done, that the scriptures of the prophets might be fulfilled, Then all the disciples forsook him, and fled" Matthew 26:56.

"Now behold, two of them were traveling that same day to a village called Emmaus, which was seven miles from Jerusalem. And they talked together of all these things which had happened" Luke 24:13-14.

One eye witness, Judas, had a tragic end. It was him who betrayed the LORD. Judas was a disciple of Jesus and a treasurer of the ministry who conspired with the Chief Priests and Captains to deliver the LORD to be crucified. When he saw the foolishness of his action, he hanged himself.

"Then Judas, which had betrayed him, when he saw that he was condemned, repented himself, and brought again the thirty pieces of silver to the chief priests and elders, Saying, I have sinned in that I have betrayed the innocent blood. And they said, What is that to us? see thou to that. And he cast down the pieces of silver in the temple, and departed, and went and hanged himself" Matthew 27:3-5.

Another set of eye witnesses was the crowd (mob) and Barabbas (a criminal whom the Bible described as a notable prisoner - Matthew 27: 16). Pilate, the Governor, had sought to release Jesus when he saw that the LORD was not guilty of any crime. It was the custom that the Governor should grant parole to a prisoner during the feast of Passover. The mob rather than have Jesus release, bargained that Barabbas be released in His stead. They ended up chanting "Let him be crucified" and cried out the more.

"But the chief priests and elders persuaded the multitude that they should ask Barabbas, and destroy Jesus. The governor answered and said unto them, whether of the twain will ye that I release unto you? They said, Barabbas. Pilate saith unto them, What shall I do then with Jesus which is called Christ? They all say unto him, Let him be crucified. And the governor said, Why, what evil hath he done? But they cried out the more, saying, Let him be crucified" Matthew 27:20-23.

"But the chief priests moved the people, that he should rather release Barabbas unto them" Mark 15:11.

Another set of eye witnesses were the dead saints who rose from their graves and appeared to many in Jerusalem, after the resurrection of the LORD. This event is breath taking as even the dead witnessed the Cross and the resurrection of the LORD, leaving the living with no excuse.

"And the graves were opened; and many bodies of the saints which slept arose, And came out of the graves after his resurrection, and went into the holy city, and appeared unto many" Matthew 27:52-53.

Scene #2: Believing The Cross

It was important that this scene be enacted so that the Cross would transcend its history. There are many in the world today who did not eye-witness the events of the Cross but who have come to believe it. I am one of those. The early disciples who witnessed the crucifixion went ahead preaching the Cross. They were instructed to preach to the whole world, beginning from Jerusalem. They passed the baton to generations of believers that today we can say that the whole world has been told of the events of the Cross.

"But ye shall receive power, after that the Holy Ghost is come upon you: and ye shall be witnesses unto me both in

Jerusalem, and in all Judaea, and in Samaria, and unto the uttermost part of the earth" Acts 1:8.

"Go ye therefore, and teach all nations, baptizing them in the name of the Father, and of the Son, and of the Holy Ghost: Teaching them to observe all things whatsoever I have commanded you: and, lo, I am with you always, even unto the end of the world. Amen" Matthew 28:19-20.

"And he said unto them, Go ye into all the world, and preach the gospel to every creature" Mark 16:15.

The early disciples, some eyewitnesses, believers or both, went about preaching the Cross. Peter, at Pentecost, made a compelling case on the Cross, citing the events of the Cross and Old Testament Prophecies to buttress his point. He summed up his sermon on the Cross to his audience in these words:

"Therefore, let all the house of Israel know assuredly, that God hath made same Jesus, whom ye have crucified, both Lord and Christ" Acts 2:36.

Three thousand persons responded to the message of the Cross and many more since then and today we have millions of believers all over the world and through the ages.

"Then they that gladly received his word were baptized: and the same day there were added unto them about three thousand souls" Acts 2:41.

Paul, the Apostle, more than any other in his time, came to embrace fully the events of the Cross and made it the cornerstone of his faith in the Lord Jesus Christ and his preaching to others, as revealed in this scripture.

"I am crucified with Christ: nevertheless, I live; yet not I, but Christ liveth in me: and the life which I now live in the flesh I live by the faith of the Son of God, who loved me, and gave himself for me" Galatians 2:20.

"But God forbid that I should glory, save in the cross of our Lord Jesus Christ, by whom the world is crucified unto me, and I unto the world" Galatians 6:14.

The Cross comes with the blessings of the LORD as evidenced in the discussion Jesus had with Thomas at His post-resurrection appearance.

"Jesus saith unto him, Thomas, because thou hast seen me, thou hast believed: blessed are they that have not seen, and yet have believed" John 20:29.

Returning To The Cross

There is a marked difference today from the days of old about the message of the Church. Today, the Church is more concerned about material wealth, miracles and building projects, among others. The preaching of the Cross is a lost coin. There is the urgent need for the Church to return to the message of the Cross as the foundation of the Gospel. The eye witnesses, especially, the disciples, who had trepidation about the Cross, went back to it after Jesus appeared to them (after His resurrection) to explain the events of the Cross. Even Thomas, the doubting disciple, had the rare opportunity of beholding the eternal Cross, thrusting his fingers into the prints of the nails on the resurrected body of the LORD.

The two disciples on the Road to Emmaus, who were disappointed at the events of the Cross, made a U-turn to Jerusalem after the LORD had expounded the truth of the Cross to them. They went ahead to preach the Cross to the other disciples who were hiding for fear of the religious establishment at the time.

> *"And they rose up the same hour, and returned to Jerusalem, and found the eleven gathered together, and them that were with them, Saying, The Lord is risen indeed, and hath appeared to Simon. And they told what things were done in the way, and how he was known of them in breaking of bread" Luke 24:33-35.*

We need to follow their example and make a U-turn to the Cross as the foundation of our faith.

At The Foot Of The Cross

CHAPTER TWO

The Power And Victory Of The Cross

Hymn: Old Rugged Cross

1. On a hill far away stood an old rugged cross,
The emblem of suff'ring and shame;
And I love that old cross where the dearest and best
For a world of lost sinners was slain.

Refrain:
So I'll cherish the old rugged cross,
Till my trophies at last I lay down;
I will cling to the old rugged cross,
And exchange it some day for a crown.

2. Oh, that old rugged cross, so despised by the world,
Has a wondrous attraction for me;
For the dear Lamb of God left His glory above
To bear it to dark Calvary.

3. In that old rugged cross, stained with blood so divine,
A wondrous beauty I see,
For 'twas on that old cross Jesus suffered and died,
To pardon and sanctify me.
4. To the old rugged cross I will ever be true;
Its shame and reproach gladly bear;
Then He'll call me some day to my home far away,
Where His glory forever I'll share.

The story of the Cross of Christ is one that must be told to all generations for what it truly represents. For therein lies the good news of the Kingdom of God. As it was then, the Cross has been misunderstood in many instances. We saw in Chapter One, how the Cross meant different things to those at the Foot of the Cross. It took further revelations of the Cross in the Epistles for the Church to gain the right perspective of the Cross and passed it down to generations of believers over the ages.

The Hymn, Old Rugged Cross, is a gentle reminder that the Cross is our trophy which will be exchanged for a crown – the very symbol of power and victory.

The Power Of The Cross

The summation of the revelation of the Cross is that the Cross is the Power of God. It was at the Cross that God's power over sin and death was displayed and satan was confounded over his foolishness for dragging mankind into sin at the Garden of Eden.

"For the preaching of the cross is to them that perish foolishness; but unto us which are saved it is the power of God" 1 Cor. 1:18.

The Cross reveals the crushing and humiliating defeat of satan, his cohorts and all that is evil. The defeat cannot be overturned by any means whatsoever. And so, the Cross stands out in time and eternity to represent POWER AND VICTORY.

"Which none of the princes of this world knew: for had they known it, they would not have crucified the Lord of glory" 1 Corinthians 2:8.

"And they overcame him by the blood of the Lamb, and by the word of their testimony; and they loved not their lives unto the death" Revelation 12:11.

During the three days and three nights in the grave, Jesus displayed the power of God, defeated satan and crushed his evil empire forever.

"Forasmuch then as the children are partakers of flesh and blood, he also himself likewise took part of the same; that through death he might destroy him that had the power of death, that is, the devil" Hebrews 2:14.

Satan was destroyed according to the scripture above through the death on the Cross and the proof of it was the resurrection of the LORD. When the LORD appeared to John as recorded in the Book of Revelation, He displayed the keys of hell and death as the proof of His conquest of satan and his evil empire.

> *"I am he that liveth, and was dead; and, behold, I am alive for evermore, Amen; and have the keys of hell and of death"* Revelation 1:18.

In my Book, The Three Silent Days and Nights, we chronicled the events that showcased the Power of the Cross, a summary of which includes:

- Jesus was quickened by the Holy Spirit. Though His body was still in the grave, He was raised up in the spirit [spiritual resurrection] to confront and defeat satan and the hosts of hell. [1 Peter 3:18-19; Psalm 16: 10-11; Ps.40:1-3;Ps.22:21;Heb.5:7;Ps.41:10-11;Ps.69:13-14,16-18].

- Jesus battled satan, principalities and the host of hell [Psalm 68:1-2; Matt.27:51(b)]

- Jesus collected the keys of hell and death from satan [Rev. 1:18]

- Jesus disarmed satan and his host, triumphed over them and made a victory parade of principalities, powers and captives of hell. [Col. 2:15; Heb. 2:14-15; Matt.12:29].

- Jesus confounded satan and his host [1 Cor.2:7-8].

- Jesus preached to spirits [fallen angels] in the underworld [1 Peter 3:18-19; 2 Peter 2:4; Jude 6] and the dead [1 Peter 4:5-6].

Understanding The Victory Of The Cross

The Victory of the Cross was hidden to mankind but made manifest through the Epistles and the preaching of the Early Disciples of the Lord Jesus Christ.

> *"Howbeit we speak wisdom among them that are perfect: yet not the wisdom of this world, nor of the princes of this world, that come to nought: But we speak the wisdom of God in a mystery, even the hidden wisdom, which God ordained before the world unto our glory: Which none of the princes of this world knew: for had they known it, they would not have crucified the Lord of glory" 1 Corinthians 2:6-8.*

The victory of the Cross of Christ is of inestimable value. It is available to all of mankind from Adam to the last man ever to be on earth; all nations, tribes, languages and people's groups;

for the dead in Christ and the living; for all of creation and nature; from eternity past to eternity future. It is a once and for all victory.

> *"And they overcame him by the blood of the Lamb, and by the word of their testimony and they loved not their lives unto the death" Revelations 12:11.*

We Have Listed Below Snippets On The Victory Of The Cross of Jesus.

Victory Of The Cross #1: Peace With God

The sacrificial death of Jesus on the Cross satisfied the righteous requirement of God for the remission of the sins of man. Mankind had sinned through Adam and fallen short of the grace of God. In the Old Testament, God allowed animal sacrifice for sin until the perfect sacrifice through the death of Jesus on the Cross. One of the benefits to mankind of the Cross of Christ was securing peace with God who had been grieved by the transgression of man (Genesis 6:5-6). In Isaiah 9:6, Jesus is named the PRINCE OF PEACE.

"But he was wounded for our transgressions, he was bruised for our iniquities: the chastisement of our peace was upon him; and with his stripes we are healed" Isaiah 53:5.

> *"And, having made peace through the blood of his cross, by him to reconcile all things unto himself; by him, I say,*

whether they be things in earth, or things in heaven" Colossians 1:20.

This victory is of foremost importance because without making peace with God, man goes no way near the blessings of God. Man was driven away from the Garden of Eden and prevented from the way of the Tree of Life (Genesis 3:22-24). It took an adequate reconciliation for man to find his way back. And that was made by the Cross of Christ.

Victory Of The Cross #2: The Indwelling Of The Holy Spirit

Having secured peace with God, God offered the very best to any penitent sinner by pouring His Spirit into the believer. This was only made possible by the substitutionary death of Jesus Christ on the Cross.

> *"In the last day, that great day of the feast, Jesus stood and cried, saying, If any man thirst, let him come unto me, and drink. He that believeth on me, as the scripture hath said, out of his belly shall flow rivers of living water. (But this spake he of the Spirit, which they that believe on him should receive: for the Holy Ghost was not yet given; because that Jesus was not yet glorified" John 7:37-39.*

The fulfillment of the above scripture came at Pentecost when the Disciples were baptised in the Holy Spirit, paving the way for all believers today to receive this gift from the Father. Jesus spoke about it before He went to the Cross and urged the Disciples to wait for the gift of the Holy Spirit from the Father (see John 15:26-27; 16:4-11; Luke 24:45-49, Acts 1:4-8).

> *"Then Peter said unto them, Repent, and be baptized every one of you in the name of Jesus Christ for the remission of sins, and ye shall receive the gift of the Holy Ghost. For the promise is unto you, and to your children, and to all that are afar off, even as many as the Lord our God shall call" Acts 2:38-39.*

> *"Now he that hath wrought us for the selfsame thing is God, who also hath given unto us the earnest of the Spirit" 2 Corinthians 5:5.*

Victory Of The Cross #3: Victory Over Flesh And Its Lust

Before the Cross, the flesh held sway on the choices men made. The flesh conspires with the power of the air to cause people to disobey God. Men walked according to the course of this world, fulfilling the desires of the flesh and of the mind.

> *"Wherein in time past ye walked according to the course of this world, according to the prince of the power of the air, the spirit that now worketh in the children of disobedience: Among whom also we all had our conversation in times past in the lusts of our flesh, fulfilling the desires of the flesh and of the mind; and were by nature the children of wrath, even as others" Ephesians 2:2-3.*

One of the proceeds of the Cross of Christ is the defeat of the lust of the flesh. By the power of the Cross, man can put his flesh under his regenerated spirit and the superintendence of the Holy Spirit. This victory could only come through the substitutionary crucifixion of the flesh of Jesus on the Cross.

> *"And they that are Christ's have crucified the flesh with the affections and lusts" Galatians 5:24.*

> *"For Christ also hath once suffered for sins, the just for the unjust, that he might bring us to God, being put to death in the flesh, but quickened by the Spirit" 1 Peter 3:18.*

> *"For as much then as Christ hath suffered for us in the flesh, arm yourselves likewise with the same mind: for he that hath suffered in the flesh hath ceased from sin; That he no longer should live the rest of his time in the flesh to the lusts of men, but to the will of God" 1 Peter 4:1-2.*

Victory Of The Cross #4: Redemption From The Curse Of The Law

The crucifixion met the legal requirement for the nullification of the curse of the law. Christ became a curse by hanging on the tree and thus provided the substitutionary remedy for all who were under the curse of the law. Christ was made a curse by crucifixion to redeem us from the curse of the law.

"Christ hath redeemed us from the curse of the law, being made a curse for us: for it is written, Cursed is everyone that hangeth on a tree: That the blessing of Abraham might come on the Gentiles through Jesus Christ; that we might receive the promise of the Spirit through faith" Galatians 3:13-14.

Victory Of The Cross #5: Victory Over Death

This is probably the most significant victory wrought by the Cross of Christ to mankind. Man was condemned to death by sin for God had said to Adam that in the day that thou eatest thereof (sin) thou shall surely die (Genesis 2:17- Emphasis Mine). This was further strengthened by the law and resulted in the decree that the soul that sinneth, it shall die (Ezekiel 18:4). Most of the laws and ordinances pronounced physical death sentences on offenders.

"For whosoever shall commit any of these abominations, even the souls that commit them shall be cut off from among their people. Therefore, shall ye keep mine ordinance, that ye commit not any one of these abominable customs, which were committed before you, and that ye defile not yourselves therein: I am the Lord your God" Leviticus 18:29-30.

Worse still, man was condemned to spiritual death as well. Even in situations where sin committed never result in instant death, every act of sin still carries the penalty of spiritual death and separation from God. It was the Cross of Christ that brought the remedy to spiritual death.

"The wages of sin is death; but the gift of God is eternal life through Jesus Christ our Lord" Romans 6:23.

"Forasmuch then as the children are partakers of flesh and blood, he also himself likewise took part of the same; that through death he might destroy him that had the power of death, that is, the devil; And deliver them who through fear of death were all their lifetime subject to bondage" Hebrews 2:14-15.

The proof of the remedy is in the resurrection of the LORD from death and the offer of the victory over death to every believer in Christ. Death is the last enemy of man that shall be finally destroyed at the resurrection of the Saints.

"The last enemy that shall be destroyed is death" Cor. 15:26.

"So when this corruptible shall have put on incorruption, and this mortal shall have put on immortality, then shall be brought to pass the saying that is written, Death is swallowed up in victory. O death, where is thy sting? O grave, where is thy victory? The sting of death is sin; and the strength of sin is the law. But thanks be to God, which giveth us the victory through our Lord Jesus Christ" 1 Corinthians 15:54-57.

Victory Of The Cross #6: Victory Over All Forces Of Evil

The Cross delivered a mortal blow to forces of evil and their hold on mankind. Evil entered the earth when Adam sinned and had prevailed until Jesus went to the Cross to deal with the sin question. His substitutionary death provided the panacea for any and every penitent sinner to extricate himself from the stronghold of sin, rendering impotent the forces of evil. Peter declared in 1 Peter 3:8 that Jesus was sent to mankind to destroy the works of the devil. He achieved this by destroying the power of sin, the principal weapon of the devil.

> *"He that committeth sin is of the devil; for the devil sinneth from the beginning. For this purpose the Son of God was manifested, that he might destroy the works of the devil" 1 Peter 3:8.*

Jesus, through the Cross delivered man from the kingdom of darkness and translated him into the kingdom of light. He spoiled principalities and powers and paraded them in a triumphant entry back into the earth at His resurrection.

> *"Blotting out the handwriting of ordinances that was against us, which was contrary to us, and took it out of the way, nailing it to his cross; And having spoiled principalities and powers, he made a shew of them openly, triumphing over them in it" Colossians 2:14-15.*

"Who hath delivered us from the power of darkness, and hath translated us into the kingdom of his dear Son: In whom we have redemption through his blood, even the forgiveness of sins" Colossians 1:13-14.

"And the angels which kept not their first estate, but left their own habitation, he hath reserved in everlasting chains under darkness unto the judgment of the great day" Jude 6.

The Nails Of The Cross

The nails of the Cross of Christ held down the things that were against us, including the Law and the handwriting of Ordinances (Colossians 2:14) and the Cup of God's Wrath (1 Thessalonians 1:10; 5:9); The nails left a physical evidence on Christ, even on His resurrected body (John 20:25-29), of the price He paid to constantly remind God of the finished work of the Cross. Jesus Christ obtained for us a legal discharge and acquittal from the judgment of the law that was against us. He vacated and disannulled the curse of the law that was hanging over mankind. When He was nailed to the Cross, the curse was nailed as well.

"Blotting out the handwriting of ordinances that was against us, which was contrary to us, and took it out of the way, nailing it to his cross" Colossians 2:14.

The LORD also took out of the way the ceremonial observances of the law, rituals of worship and rules which were a yoke to the Jews and a partition wall to the Gentiles. This victory can only come by the symbolism of the nails. The victory is reminiscent of the ancient methods of cancelling a bond, either by crossing the writing or striking it through with a nail (Matthew Henry Commentary on Colossians 2:14).

The song by Jim Reeves, "I'd rather have Jesus", reveals in the 1st stanza the importance of being led by the nail-pierced hand of the LORD:

> I'd rather have Jesus than silver or gold;
> I'd rather be His than have riches untold;
> I'd rather have Jesus than houses or lands;
> I'd rather be led by His nail-pierced hand.
>
> *Refrain:*
> *Than to be the king of a vast domain*
> *Or be held in sin's dread sway;*
> *I'd rather have Jesus than anything*
> *This world affords today.*

Enforcing The Victory Of The Cross

One may ask why there is still so much evil ravaging the world today even after the victory the LORD wrought at the Cross. The reason is simple. Christ has won for us an eternal victory that the Church is called to enforce in time. We are not fighting to win but to sustain the victory on this side of eternity. Satan is a defeated foe who knows that his time to exit the arena is short (Revelation 12:12).

Therefore, we are called to enforce the victory of the Cross in our everyday encounter with the forces of evil here on earth. Living the substitutionary life of Christ here on earth is the most potent weapon for enforcing the victory of the Cross. Satan is afraid of any one who looks like Jesus.

> *"I am crucified with Christ: nevertheless I live; yet not I, but Christ liveth in me: and the life which I now live in the flesh I live by the faith of the Son of God, who loved me, and gave himself for me" Galatians 2:20.*

The substitutionary life is for man to die to self-will and allow Christ to control his life. Paul said of this that it is Christ that lives in him. So, should we all come to the point of faith where only Christ calls all the shots. Paul went on to tell the Church that our life is hid with Christ in God. That way our entire life is Christ. When we live this way, victory is assured, and the Cross is enforced.

> *"For ye are dead, and your life is hid with Christ in God. When Christ, who is our life, shall appear, then shall ye also appear with him in glory" Colossians 3:3-4.*

Many believers know Jesus as the Christ but struggle with the Crucified Christ (Matt.16:21-25). There would be no

Christianity without the Cross for it is the source of its good news, power (1 Corinthians.1:18), glory and crown (1 Peter 4:13). The mindset of the Cross forms the foundation of the Christian attitude (Philippians 2:5-11) In deed, the Cross is the very basis for Christian living (Galatians 2:20). The Cross is our footstep (1 Peter 2:21). Ultimately, Christ is coming for the crucified Church (Colossians 3:1-4).

Let's bear the marks of the Cross of Christ (Galatians 6:17) to evidence His blood-bought victory for us. It is for such that we are called to (Galatians 6:14-16). Amen.

Song: BY YOUR BLOOD
By Your Blood, You Crushed Principalities
Jesus, Jesus
By Your Name, Establish Authority
Jesus, Jesus, The Righteous.

Refrain:
Jesus, Jesus, Jesus
Your Reign Over All
Jesus, Jesus, Jesus
You Reign Over All

CHAPTER THREE

The Glory Of The Cross

Hymn: NEAR THE CROSS (Frances J. Crosby)

1. Jesus, keep me near the cross,
There a precious fountain—
Free to all, a healing stream—
Flows from Calv'ry's mountain.

Refrain:
In the cross, in the cross,
Be my glory ever;
Till my raptured soul shall find
Rest beyond the river.

2. Near the cross, a trembling soul,
Love and Mercy found me;
There the bright and morning star
Sheds its beams around me.

3. Near the cross! O Lamb of God,
Bring its scenes before me;
Help me walk from day to day,
With its shadows o'er me.

4. Near the cross I'll watch and wait
Hoping, trusting ever,
Till I reach the golden strand,
Just beyond the river.

The Hymn, Near the Cross by Frances J. Crosby, always reminds us of the glory of the Cross. Its wonderful lines like "In the cross ... be my glory ever; ...Till I reach the golden strand...", beckons on us to go beyond the veil of Calvary Hill and behold the golden throne that we will share with the LORD in eternity - all because of what Jesus accomplished at the Cross. In this chapter, we will walk the road to Emmaus, where Jesus, after His resurrection, met two of His disciples who were discouraged at the events of the Cross. They left Jerusalem in disappointment, but the LORD met them on the way and offered a glimpse into the pathway from the Cross to Glory.

No Short Cut to Glory

In his comfort zone, man lives in a utopia. Man would rather expect a crown without a thorn. Therefore, it was natural for the disciples to see Jesus' earthly ministry as a comfort zone. When confronted with the idea of the Messiah going to the Cross, they could not accept it. Each time the LORD, raised the issue of His imminent death on the Cross, the disciples took the easy road of earthly rulership and the benefits such would convey on them. Peter even rebuked the LORD concerning His impending death on the Cross.

> *"From that time forth began Jesus to shew unto his disciples, how that he must go unto Jerusalem, and suffer many things of the elders and chief priests and scribes, and be killed, and be raised again the third day. Then Peter took him, and began to rebuke him, saying, Be it far from thee, Lord: this shall not be unto thee. But he turned, and said unto Peter, Get thee behind me, Satan: thou art an offence unto me: for thou savourest not the things that be of God, but those that be of men" Matthew 16:21-23.*

Most of the disciples fled from the scene of the Cross and two of them even relocated to Emmaus. They summed their disappointment in the Cross in these words: *"But we trusted that it had been he which should have redeemed Israel: and beside all this, today is the third day since these things were done."*

> *"And he said unto them, What things? And they said unto him, Concerning Jesus of Nazareth, which was a prophet mighty in deed and word before God and all the people: And how the chief priests and our rulers delivered him to be condemned to death, and have crucified him. But we trusted that it had been he which should have redeemed Israel: and beside all this, today is the third day since these things were done" Luke 24:19-21.*

Man would prefer gains without pains, profit without loss, power without problems, prize without price, and glory without the Cross. This mindset is contrary to nature. For nature teaches us that for every flower there is a thorn and so it should be expected that the Cross would produce glory. This was the point that the LORD made to the two disciples on the road to Emmaus. And He made it in very strong terms that could possibly be made.

> *"Then he said unto them, O fools, and slow of heart to believe all that the prophets have spoken: Ought not Christ to have suffered these things, and to enter into his glory?"*
> *Luke 24:25-26.*

The rhetorical question, "Ought not Christ to have suffered these things, and to enter into his glory?", dealt a blow to the comfort zone mindset of the disciples and brought them back to the conclusion that there was no short cut to glory. No prayer (Luke 22:42) or strong crying (Hebrew 5:5-9) can shorten the journey to the throne of glory but obedience (Hebrew 5:8-9; Phil 2:8-9) is the only pathway to the throne of glory. The Cross symbolises the sacrificial obedience of Jesus to the Father. Today, He sits on the right hand of God in glory, having passed through the Cross. And such is expected of His Disciples.

> *"But this man, after he had offered one sacrifice for sins forever, sat down on the right hand of God"* Hebrews 10:12.

"Looking unto Jesus the author and finisher of our faith; who for the joy that was set before him endured the cross, despising the shame, and is set down at the right hand of the throne of God" Hebrews 12:2.

The Glory of Christ

The rhetorical question, "Ought not Christ to have suffered these things, and to enter into his glory?", unveils the Cross. The Cross is the pathway to Glory. Jesus had sought from the Father to enter into glory after the Cross. He prayed earnestly for it in John 17:4-5

"I have glorified thee on the earth: I have finished the work which thou gavest me to do. And now, O Father, glorify thou me with thine own self with the glory which I had with thee before the world was" John 17:4-5.

Notice that Jesus predicated His request for the glory on the work He did on earth and finished. He had said in John 19:30, "It is Finished". The Cross is the sum of His work.

"After this, Jesus knowing that all things were now accomplished, that the scripture might be fulfilled, saith, I thirst. Now there was set a vessel full of vinegar: and they filled a spunge with vinegar, and put it upon hyssop, and put it to his mouth. When Jesus therefore had received the vinegar, he said, It is finished: and he bowed his head, and gave up the ghost" John 19:28-30.

"And Jesus answered them, saying, The hour is come, that the Son of man should be glorified...Now is my soul troubled; and what shall I say? Father, save me from this hour: but for this cause came I unto this hour. Father, glorify thy name. Then came there a voice from heaven, saying, I have both glorified it, and will glorify it again" John 12:23,27-28.

Jesus' reference to the hour of His glorification was the Cross as can be seen in the scriptures above. The Father affirmed that the glory was His to receive. It is evident that all the glory the LORD got back from the Father was dependent on His death on the Cross. But what is this glory? Jesus, after the Cross, resurrected and ascended to the Throne of God, now sitting at the right hand of God in glory. Scriptures have given us a glimpse of the throne of His glory.

"And immediately I was in the spirit: and behold, a throne was set in heaven...and there was rainbow round the throne, in sight like unto an emerald...and before the throne there was a sea of glass like unto crystal..." Revelations 4:1-11.

"And I saw a great white throne, and He that sat on it, from whose face the earth and the heaven fled away...and He that sat upon the throne said, Behold I make all things new...and he shew me a pure river of water of life, clear as crystal, proceeding out of the throne of God" Revelations 20:11; 21:5; 22:1.

"And there shall be no more curse: but the throne of God and of the Lamb shall be in it; and His servants shall serve Him: and they shall see His face; and His name shall be in their foreheads…and they shall reign for ever and ever" Revelations 22:3-5.

The throne of glory and the privileges of sitting as King and Judge on the throne is the sum of the glory that Jesus entered into after the Cross.

"When the Son of man shall come in his glory, and all the holy angels with him, then shall he sit upon the throne of his glory" Matthew 25:31.

"But he, being full of the Holy Ghost, looked up steadfastly into heaven, and saw the glory of God and Jesus standing on the right hand of God" Acts 7:55-60.

This song comes handy to remind us of the glory of Christ and need for us to proclaim the glory of the Risen LORD, who once was slain to reconcile man to God.

ALL HEAVENS DECLARE
All heavens declare
The glory of the risen Lord
Who can compare
With the beauty of the Lord

Refrain
Forever, You will be

The Lamb upon the throne
I gladly bow my knees
And worship You alone

I will proclaim
The glory of the risen Lord
Who once was slain
To reconcile man to God

Sharing the Glory of Christ

Jesus is on the throne, making intercession for the Church (Romans 8:34), reigning over all and preparing a glorious Church (Ephesians 5:27). One day, we will sit with Christ around the Throne.

> *"And Jesus said unto them, Verily I say unto you, That ye which have followed me, in the regeneration when the Son of man shall sit in the throne of his glory, ye also shall sit upon twelve thrones, judging the twelve tribes of Israel"* *Matthew 19:28.*

> *"To him that overcometh will I grant to sit with me in my throne, even as I also overcame, and am set down with my Father in his throne"* *Revelation 3:21.*

> *"Father, I will that they also, whom thou hast given me, be with me where I am; that they may behold my glory, which thou hast given me: for thou lovedst me before the foundation of the world"* *John 17:24.* (Emphasis Mine)

We are called to glory. This is the inheritance embedded in the call of God upon believers. We are called to obtain the glory of Jesus Christ. This means that Jesus will share His glory with His bride, the Church.

> *"That ye would walk worthy of God, who hath called you unto his kingdom and glory" 1 Thessalonians 2:12.*

> *"Whereunto he called you by our gospel, to the obtaining of the glory of our Lord Jesus Christ" 2 Thessalonians 2:14.* (Emphasis Mine)

In the Cross we see the glory of Christ. Therefore, to share the glory we must share the Cross. For it is in the Cross that we have a part in the glory of Christ.

> *"But the God of all grace, who hath called us unto his eternal glory by Christ Jesus, after that ye have suffered a while, make you perfect, stablish, strengthen, settle you" 1 Peter 5:10.* (Emphasis Mine)

In the above scripture, note how Peter preconditioned the eternal glory of believers with the finished work of the Cross in the believers. Paul alluded to this when he unveiled the mystery of salvation. It is Christ in us (the finished work of the Cross) that is the hope of glory.

"Even the mystery which hath been hid from ages and from generations, but now is made manifest to his saints: To whom God would make known what is the riches of the glory of this mystery among the Gentiles; which is Christ in you, the hope of glory" Colossians 1:26-27.

We are called to follow the Lord Jesus' steps in suffering for righteousness sake (1 Peter 2:21). This is not self-appointed suffering but suffering from the surrender of our personal and self-will for the supremacy of the perfect will of God. Jesus laid down His will for the will of the Father on the Cross. The Cross is a perfect example how the will of man is crossed out by the will of God. Jesus prayed earnestly at the Garden of Gethsemane for the Cross to pass by Him but ultimately bowed to the supremacy of the will of God in these words – "Thy will be done" (Matthew 26:42). We are not to suffer as murderers (for our faults). We are to bless them that cause us sufferings (Matt.5:10).

Sufferings prepare us for growth and maturity and should be accepted as the Lord's will, not by our own will. The prophets and disciples of old are examples for Christians suffering today (James 5:10; Heb.11).

"For to you it has been granted on behalf of Christ, not only to believe in Him, but also to suffer for His sake" Philippians 1:29.

The lesson for today's believers is: No Cross (emblem of suffering and shame) No Glory!

"And if children, then heirs; heirs of God, and joint-heirs with Christ; if so be that we suffer with him, that we may be also glorified together. For I reckon that the sufferings of this present time are not worthy to be compared with the glory which shall be revealed in us" (Romans 8:17-18).

At The Foot Of The Cross

CHAPTER FOUR

The Sufficiency Of The Cross

Hymn: My Jesus I Love Thee

My Jesus, I love Thee, I know Thou art mine;
For Thee all the follies of sin, I resign;
My gracious Redeemer, my Saviour art Thou;
If ever I loved Thee, my Jesus, 'tis now.

I love Thee because Thou hast first loved me,
And purchased my pardon on Calvary's tree;
I love Thee for wearing the thorns on Thy brow;
If ever I loved Thee, my Jesus, 'tis now.

I'll love Thee in life, I will love Thee in death,
And praise Thee as long as Thou lendest me breath;
And say when the death dew lies cold on my brow,
If ever I loved Thee, my Jesus, 'tis now.

In mansions of glory and endless delight,
I'll ever adore Thee in heaven so bright;
I'll sing with the glittering crown on my brow,
If ever I loved Thee, my Jesus, 'tis now.

The Hymn, My Jesus I love Thee, draws us to the love mark for the LORD. This is more compelling when we come to terms with the price and prize of the Cross. I like the lines, "I love Thee for wearing the thorns on Thy brow; If ever I loved Thee, my Jesus, 'tis now". Then we move to the sufficiency of the Cross with lines such as "In mansions of glory and endless delight, I'll ever adore Thee in heaven so bright; I'll sing with the glittering crown on my brow, If ever I loved Thee, my Jesus, 'tis now." The Cross is all we need from God for it is in the Cross that the love of God, the riches of His inheritance, glory and grace are bound up as a gift to man.

We must come to the point in our journey of faith where we can conclude without any equivocation that the crucifixion of the LORD is epicentral to all we can and will ever receive from God. If Christ was born without facing the Cross, then the penalty for sin would not have been paid for. And He could not have resurrected without the Cross. He could not have ascended without the Cross. Indeed, the summary of the Gospel is Christ hath died, Christ hath risen and Christ will come again.

"He that descended is the same also that ascended up far above all heavens, that he might fill all things" Ephesians 4:10.

For Christ to fill all things, he descended (by reason of the death on the Cross) and then ascended. The Cross sets Jesus apart from other personalities, prophets, religious figures and men of faith. Peter made a compelling case about the Cross at Pentecost and persuaded his audience with these words:

"Men and brethren, let me freely speak unto you of the patriarch David, that he is both dead and buried, and his sepulchre is with us unto this day. Therefore being a prophet, and knowing that God had sworn with an oath to him, that of the fruit of his loins, according to the flesh, he would raise up Christ to sit on his throne; He seeing this before spake of the resurrection of Christ, that his soul was not left in hell, neither his flesh did see corruption. This Jesus hath God raised up, whereof we all are witnesses. Therefore being by the right hand of God exalted, and having received of the Father the promise of the Holy Ghost, he hath shed forth this, which ye now see and hear. For David is not ascended into the heavens: but he saith himself, The Lord said unto my Lord, Sit thou on my right hand, Until I make thy foes thy footstool. Therefore let all the house of Israel know assuredly, that God hath made that same Jesus, whom ye have crucified, both Lord and Christ" Acts 2:29-36. (Emphasis Mine)

The Cross was the central message and focal point of the

early disciples and should be ours today. Paul, more than any other in his time, made the Cross the centre of life, ministry and focus in these words:

"For I determined not to know anything among you, save Jesus Christ, and him crucified" 1 Corinthians 2:2.

Paul made the Cross the centre of his ministry. There was something Paul knew about the Cross that propelled his curiosity to set aside all other aspects of ministry and focused on "Jesus Christ, and Him crucified". Not Jesus Christ or Christ crucified but Jesus Christ and Him crucified, giving effect of the Cross on the ministry of Jesus Christ.

"If in this life only we have hope in Christ, we are of all men most miserable. But now is Christ risen from the dead, and become the firstfruits of them that slept" 2 Corinthians 15:19-20.

The anchor of our faith is the finished work of the Cross. Everywhere he ministered, Paul made a case for the Cross. He knew that the Christian experience is made real by how we see Jesus on the Cross. In Hebrews 2:9 the expression, But we see Jesus, is a call for deeper insight into the events of the Cross.

"But we see Jesus, who was made a little lower than the angels for the suffering of death, crowned with glory and honour; that he by the grace of God should taste death for every man" Hebrew 2:9.

In this chapter we will examine the sufficiency of the Cross through the lens of the Gospel that Christ hath died, Christ hath risen and Christ will come again. We will see how Christ's Ministry as the Door (Christ hath died), the Way (Christ hath risen again) and the End (Christ will come again) have met all that man will ever need beyond time and eternity, and hence the sufficiency of the Cross. For the Cross is the Door for all that man can receive in Christ.

Seeing the Crucified Christ Is all We Need

In their book, "Seeing Jesus", Roy and Revel Hession affirmed that:

"To create, God had to speak, and it was done. But to redeem, He had to bleed. And He did so in the Person of His Son, Jesus Christ, whom He sent to take the place of death upon the Cross which our sin had so richly deserved."

Redemption was no last-minute thought, brought into being to meet an unexpected emergency. No sooner had sin entered the garden than God spoke of Christ who was to come and who was to bruise the serpent's (that is, satan's) head, His own heel being bruised (at the Cross) in the process (Genesis

3:15). We will expound on this in Chapter Seven under the theme: The Eternal Cross. But suffice to say at this point, that the eternal dimension of the Cross makes the Crucified Christ all that we needed, need and will ever need. We must see the Crucified Christ as such. We are convinced that this was the reason for Paul's declaration that the Crucified Christ was his preference above all else:

"For I determined not to know anything among you, save Jesus Christ, and him crucified" 1 Corinthians 2:2.

The reason that the Crucified Christ is above all else we will ever need is His divinity plus His humanity and the Cross. For the eternal Cross to be manifest in time, Jesus became man so that He could taste death and redeem man from sin. In His divinity, He could not taste death, the very penalty for sin. But in His humanity, He fulfilled the righteous requirement for a ransom for sin, which is death.

"Forasmuch then as the children are partakers of flesh and blood, he also himself likewise took part of the same; that through death he might destroy him that had the power of death, that is, the devil; And deliver them who through fear of death were all their lifetime subject to bondage. For verily he took not on him the nature of angels; but he took on him the seed of Abraham. Wherefore in all things it behoved him to be made like unto his brethren, that he might be a merciful and faithful high priest in things pertaining to

God, to make reconciliation for the sins of the people. For in that he himself hath suffered being tempted, he is able to succour them that are tempted" Hebrews 2:14-18.

Jesus Christ alone and Him alone met the condition for the redemption of man. He did that on the Cross. As important as His divinity was, it was necessary for Him to be made in the likeness of man to be able to taste death and destroy the power of the devil over sinful man. No man or angel or principality could have mediated between God and man concerning God's judgment, except by the Cross. Only Jesus Christ did it! And Him alone is our sufficiency.

"For there is one God, and one mediator between God and men, the man Christ Jesus; Who gave himself a ransom for all, to be testified in due time" 1 Timothy 2:5-6.

"How much more shall the blood of Christ, who through the eternal Spirit offered himself without spot to God, purge your conscience from dead works to serve the living God? And for this cause he is the mediator of the new testament, that by means of death, for the redemption of the transgressions that were under the first testament, they which are called might receive the promise of eternal inheritance" Hebrews 9:15-16.

Now let's look at the divinity of Christ. We have seen His humanity leading Him to the Cross. Let's us consider His divinity leading Him to the earth. According to Roy and Revel Hession in their Book, Seeing Jesus, 'One of the most breath-taking occasions when Jesus claimed equality with the Father was when He said, "Before Abraham was, I am" (John 8:58). The sentence immediately challenges our attention because of the extraordinary liberty it takes with our grammar. If the Lord Jesus had merely wanted to express His pre-existence, He would surely have said, "Before Abraham was, I was". But He says, "Before Abraham was, I AM". Without any doubt He is taking us back to that day when Moses, bowing before God at the burning bush, asked what name he should give the God who was sending him to the children of Israel. God's reply then was, 1 AM THAT I AM' (Exodus 3:14-15). Therefore, when the Lord Jesus said this word to the Jews, He was daring to claim to be the great I AM of the Old Testament, whom they all knew to be the Covenant God of their fathers. He went even further, asserting that their eternal destiny would depend on their accepting Him as such, for, said He, "If ye believe not that I AM, ye shall die in your sins" (John 8:24).

The meaning of this great name, Jehovah, that is I AM, which Jesus claimed for Himself, is twofold. It means first of all that He is the Ever-present One, who stands outside of time, to whom there is no past or future but to whom everything is present. Clearly, that is the first meaning of this strange mixture of tenses..." Before Abraham was, I AM." And that surely is what eternity is – not merely elongated time, but another realm altogether where everything is one glorious present. What a vision this gives of our Lord Jesus, the Eternal One, the I AM! To Him our lives with their past and future are all present; our yesterdays as well as our tomorrows are all now to Him.

The name, I AM of Jehovah, is an unfinished sentence. It has no object. I am- what? Great is the wonder when we discover, as we continue with our Bibles, that He is saying," I AM, whatever My people need in Me", and that the sentence is purposely left blank so that man may bring his many and various needs, as they arise, to complete it! The name, Jehovah, is like a blank cheque. Do you lack peace? "I am thy peace", says He. Do you lack strength? "I am thy strength". Do you lack spiritual life? "I am thy life". Do you lack wisdom? "I am thy wisdom", and so on. Sometimes in the Old Testament, this blank cheque is filled for us, to encourage us to fill in ourselves as we need in the New Testament.

Every now and then we come across "Jehovah" compounded with another word to form His completed name for that occasion. The seven wonderful revelations of the compound name of Jehovah in the Old Testament are: Jehovah-Nissi – "I am thy banner" (Exodus 17:15); Jehovah-Shalom – "I am thy peace" (Judges 6:24); Jehovah Tsidkenu-"I am thy righteousness" (Jeremiah 23:6); Jehovah Rohi- "I am thy shepherd" (Psalm 23:1); Jehovah-Jireh –"I am the One who provides" (Genesis 22:14); Jehovah-Rapha –"I am the One who heals" (Exodus 15:26); and Jehovah-Shammah-"I am the One who is present" (Ezekiel 48:35).

When it came to meeting His people's need as sinners, it had to be Jesus. There was no other way. There was no other good enough to pay the price of sin. And God did not withhold Him. But God, in giving Him to be the answer to our sin, has given Him to be the answer to all our other needs, spiritual, moral and material.

> *"He that spared not his own Son, but delivered him up for us all, how shall he not with him also freely give us all things?" Romans 8:32.*

Jesus thus takes into Himself all the meanings of the Old Testament compound names of Jehovah, fulfilling and eclipsing them all in the final compound name He bears, "JESUS: I am thy salvation". The name, "Jesus", is the Greek form of the Hebrew name, "Jehoshua". The first letters of this name, "Je" are a contraction of "Jehovah" and are linked with a Hebrew name meaning "salvation" to make the full name "Jehovah is salvation" (Roy and Revel Hession, 1950).

Let's end this section with the song, "Lord You are Everything to me" as our confession and profession of the sufficiency of the Cross of Christ.

Song: Lord you are Everything to me
Everything (2x)
Lord you are Everything to me (Sing it again)
Everything (2x)
Lord You are Everything to me (2x)

My treasure, my priority
Who can compare to You
Great is the measure of Your royalty
O morning stars You truly are
Everything to me
Lord… You are Everything to us Lord

Let us see the sufficiency of the crucified Christ in the claim by Jesus that He is the Door (Christ hath died), the Way (Christ hath risen again) and the End (Christ will come again) and how the Cross played a crucial role in the fulfilment of these claims:

Seeing the Crucified Christ as the Door

Jesus made a very profound declaration in John 10:9 about Himself as the Door:

> *"I AM the Door: by me if any man enter in, he shall be saved, and shall go in and out, and find pasture" John 10:9.*

Here the LORD Jesus confronts us with another great "I AM". He is the Door to the excluded. All have sinned and come short of the glory of God (Romans 3:23). When Adam sinned in the Garden of Eden, he and Eve (all mankind) were excluded from the tree of life. Since then man lives the life of the 'East of the garden.'

> *"Therefore the LORD God sent him forth from the garden of Eden, to till the ground from whence he was taken. So he drove out the man; and he placed at the east of the garden of Eden Cherubims, and a flaming sword which turned every way, to keep the way of the tree of life"* Genesis 3:23-24.

For man to find his way to God, he needs to go through the Door. Christ is the Door to the salvation of man, easily assessible by any man (the weakest and most failing to the saintliest). Christ is the Door to revival and every other blessings for the Christian as He is the Door to salvation for the lost.

The fact that the LORD referred to Himself as the Door, presupposes that there is a wall, a barrier, which excludes man from God. For when Adam sinned, God set the flaming sword to bar the way to the Tree of Life in the Garden of Eden (Genesis 3:34). Sin always builds a wall between man and God.

> *"But your iniquities have separated between you and your God, and your sins have hid his face from you, that he will not hear"* Isaiah 59:2.

Since Adam, all are born East of Eden until they find Jesus, the Door back to Paradise. Jesus' ministry as the Door was perfected on the Cross when the veil of the temple was torn apart, making it possible for any vile sinner (Jews and Gentiles) to come to God by repentance.

"Jesus, when he had cried again with a loud voice, yielded up the ghost. And, behold, the veil of the temple was rent in twain from the top to the bottom; and the earth did quake, and the rocks rent;" Matthew 27:50-51.

The symbolic renting of the veil opens the way to the Holy of Holies. The veil of the temple, which for centuries had hung as an excluding barrier between the Holy of Holies and the rest of the temple, having been rent declared the door for sinful man open. We are now urged to have "boldness to enter the Holiest by the blood of Jesus, by a new and living way."

"Having therefore, brethren, boldness to enter into the holiest by the blood of Jesus, By a new and living way, which he hath consecrated for us, through the veil, that is to say, his flesh; And having an high priest over the house of God; Let us draw near with a true heart in full assurance of faith, having our hearts sprinkled from an evil conscience, and our bodies washed with pure water. Let us hold fast the profession of our faith without wavering; (for he is faithful that promised;)" Hebrews 10:19-23.

Jesus does not merely show us a door, He is the Door. We must see Him as the Open Door, to both Jews and Gentiles. He is also a Narrow Door, fit for every man at a personal level. If you are going to enter, you will have to stand there utterly alone. At first the road to the Cross seems broad (all are invited) but gets narrow at repentance (sinner must stand alone to repent). It must be you alone who repents, without waiting for any other (Matthew 7:14).

This again marks the sufficiency of the Cross of Christ for it authenticates the ministry of Jesus as the Door to sinners and the saints.

Seeing The Crucified Christ As The Way

Another profound statement Jesus made about Himself and how the Cross authenticated it is "I AM the Way."

> *"Jesus saith unto him, I AM the way, the truth, and the life: no man cometh unto the Father, but by me" John 14:6.*

The picture of the Lord Jesus as the Door properly belongs to the beginning of the Christian life. It is also the entrance of the believer to the blessedness of the kingdom of God. But what lies beyond the Door? Scripture gives us the picture of the Door leading us not into a house or garden but onto a path (Matthew 7:14). The path opens unto a way that stretches right ahead. And the Lord Jesus who had said, "I AM the Door" now says, "I AM the Way" (John 14:6) that lies beyond the Door. Both Door and Way are the same blessed Person, Jesus Christ. The ministry of Jesus as the Way means a continuous walk with Him by every believer who has come through the Door. The "Way" means there is a path to walk with Jesus Christ. God who provided for us the Door has not failed to provide the well-marked pathway (the Way of Holiness) we so much need after we have entered by the Door (Isaiah 35:8-9). Christ is the Way to every experience of the believer in God's kingdom.

It is not His life nor His teaching that made the Lord Jesus the Door, but rather His Cross, His blood, His finished work for sin. It is the same blood and finished work that constitutes Him the Way for us. Indeed, in Hebrews 10 the new and living way into the Holy of Holies of God's presence is clearly stated to be by the blood of Jesus.

> "Having therefore, brethren, boldness to enter into the holiest by the blood of Jesus, By a new and living way, which he hath consecrated for us, through the veil, that is to say, his flesh; And having an high priest over the house of God; Let us draw near with a true heart in full assurance of faith, having our hearts sprinkled from an evil conscience, and our bodies washed with pure water" Hebrews 10:19-22. (Emphasis Mine)

This again marks the sufficiency of the Cross of Christ for it authenticates the ministry of Jesus as the Way to believers.

Seeing The Crucified Christ As The End

In the previous section, we saw Jesus as the Way by reason of the Cross. We must now ask ourselves, where does the Way lead to? What is its end? The natural thing is for us to think that the Way will lead us to being made powerful, being used in winning souls, large church attendance, spiritual success or even revival. We all get it wrong by imagining the end that Christianity faith conveys on man! We imagine rapture or end of time (age) as the ultimate a believer can attain. Jesus went to the Cross for something more than these. Let's revisit John 14:6:

> *"Jesus saith unto him, I AM the way, the truth, and the life: no man cometh unto the Father, but by me" John 14:6.*

Arising from the statement above, we can see the interplay of the Way and the End. Permit me to paraphrase John 14:6, thus:

> *"I AM the Way…No one comes to the Father (End) but by Me (The Way). John 14:6. (Emphasis Mine)*

Remember that Jesus made this profound statement in answer to a question by Thomas, one of the disciples. Thomas had sought to know the way to where Jesus was going.

> *"Thomas saith unto him, Lord, we know not whither thou goest; and how can we know the way?" John 14:5.*

Jesus went further and deeper to present the interface between the Way and End in Himself when He said, "If ye had known me, ye should have known my Father also: and from henceforth ye know him, and have seen him (John 14:7). Another disciple, Philip, joined the conversation by asking Him to show them the Father. To this Jesus said:

> "Jesus saith unto him, Have I been so long time with you, and yet hast thou not known me, Philip? he that hath seen me hath seen the Father; and how sayest thou then, Shew us the Father? Believest thou not that I am in the Father, and the Father in me? the words that I speak unto you I speak not of myself: but the Father that dwelleth in me, he doeth the works" John 14:9-10.

Permit me to paraphrase Philip's question and the LORD's answer, thus:

> "Show us the Father (End)…He who has seen Me (The Way) has seen the Father (The End)" John 14:8-9. (Emphasis Mine)

By this statement, Jesus was saying that He is both the Way and the End. In other words, Jesus was saying that the "I AM" of the Old Testament is the "I AM" of the New Testament (see John 14:11; 8:58; 1:18). In finding Him, men have not only found the Way but the End too. We do not have to go beyond Him to something else to satisfy our needs. He is the end of all we need, and the simple, easily accessible Way to that End. Our End is to be the Lord Jesus Himself. Scripture tells us that the whole purpose of Jesus on the Cross was to reconcile us "unto Himself."

"To wit, that God was in Christ, reconciling the world unto himself, not imputing their trespasses unto them; and hath committed unto us the word of reconciliation" 2 Corinthians 5:19. (Emphasis Mine)

"Looking for that blessed hope, and the glorious appearing of the great God and our Saviour Jesus Christ; Who gave himself for us, that he might redeem us from all iniquity, and purify unto himself a peculiar people, zealous of good works" Titus 2:13-14. (Emphasis Mine)

"For whatever Man may need, Jesus says, "I AM ALPHA AND OMEGA, the Beginning and the End..." (see Revelations 1:8; 21:6; 22:13).

In summary, Jesus Christ is THE DOOR, THE WAY AND THE END. He achieved this through His sacrificial death on the Cross. The Cross is sufficient for all of the needs of man. This was what emboldened Paul to declare to the Corinthian Church, "For I determined not to know anything among you, save Jesus Christ, and him crucified."-1 Corinthians 2:2. We all should come to the same point of faith where we boldly declare the Cross as the epicentre of our new life in Christ and everything we do. The Church is called to the Cross and not apart from it. For without the Cross, Christianity is doomed and powerless.

> *"And my speech and my preaching was not with enticing words of man's wisdom, but in demonstration of the Spirit and of power: That your faith should not stand in the wisdom of men, but in the power of God" 1 Corinthians 2:4-5.*

What do we have today in the Church? Enticing words of man's wisdom, motivation speeches, stardom, advertising stunts, media hypes, publicity, talking points and wisdom of men have invaded the pulpit and believers don't know what to believe again. In all of these, one thing is lacking, the power of God, and these preachers know that! That is why some of them go to the ridiculous extent of manufacturing and advertising miracles to deceive people and cover up their despicable lack of connection to the powerhouse of God – The Cross. They don't understand that the power of God is made manifest in the preaching of the Cross and not in the enticing words of man's wisdom.

Again, we warn the Church to go back to the Cross and she will do well to embark on a U-Turn if she must be relevant in the world of lost sinners today.

These sections rely on materials from the book, "Seeing Jesus" by Roy and Revel Mession.

CHAPTER FIVE

Counting The Cost

Song: Here I am to Worship
Here I am to worship; Here I am to bow down
Here I am to say that, You are my God
Altogether lovely, altogether worthy, altogether wonderful to me. (x3)

 I never knew how much it cost to see my sins upon that cross (x3)

Here I am to worship; Here I am to bow down
Here I am to say that, You are my God
Altogether lovely, altogether worthy, altogether wonderful to me.

Song: Follow Me
1. Jesus Says, "Follow Me"
"Follow Me"
Take up your Cross and follow Me

2. I say to my Lord
I'll follow You (2cc)
I'll take up my Cross and
Follow You

The two songs above bring home the message that there is a price tag to the Cross of Christ. The Cross is an expensive gift from God to man: it cost God the death of His only begotten Son. Jesus paid a debt He did not owe because we owed a debt we could not pay. Having paid the price at the Cross, the LORD made a demand on believers to take up the Cross and follow Him. He is invariably asking us to count the cost of the Cross as we attempt to follow Him. He is also asking us to carefully consider and accept the demands of the Cross on our lives in this world of lost sinners. Between coming to the saving grace offered by Jesus and following Him, there is a Cross. The Cross is first and foremost a cost or a price. That is why believers are asked to count the cost.

"And whosoever doth not bear his cross, and come after me, cannot be my disciple. For which of you, intending to build a tower, sitteth not down first, and counteth the cost, whether he have sufficient to finish it? Lest haply, after he hath laid the foundation, and is not able to finish it, all that behold it begin to mock him, Saying, This man began to build, and was not able to finish" Luke 14:27–30. (Emphasis Mine)

We are also called to a life that conforms with the Cross by the fellowship with Christ's sufferings. This places a great demand on our lives. Our lives are meant to be wrapped around the price of the Cross. In other words, we are meant to live a crucified life. For I reckon that life lived outside the Cross of Christ is life at cross-purpose with God. The Cross is everything to a sinner as well as a saint. That is what Paul meant by his declaration to the Philippian Church in these words:

> *"But what things were gain to me, those I counted loss for Christ. Yea doubtless, and I count all things but loss for the excellency of the knowledge of Christ Jesus my Lord: for whom I have suffered the loss of all things, and do count them but dung, that I may win Christ, And be found in him, not having mine own righteousness, which is of the law, but that which is through the faith of Christ, the righteousness which is of God by faith: That I may know him, and the power of his resurrection, and the fellowship of his sufferings, being made conformable unto his death"*
> *Philippians 3:7-10.*

Paul's whole life was centred around the Cross of Christ. He considered dung, everything outside the Cross. He suffered the loss of all things and counted them dung. He did all these to be made conformed unto the death of Christ (the Cross). And so, should we!

Why would a believer subject himself to the Cross of Christ? Why would he accept the fellowship of His suffering (the

Cross) as a lifestyle? Paul knew something that the Church today needs to learn along: that the proceed of the Cross is the glory (Luke 24:26).

"Ought not Christ to have suffered these things, and to enter into his glory?" Luke 24:26.

The Cross is both a price and a prize. The Cross is firstly a trophy to the Risen LORD from God, the Father and secondly a trophy from the Risen LORD to His blood bought bride. The Cross is our sufficiency as discussed in Chapter Four.

"If by any means I might attain unto the resurrection of the dead.... I press toward the mark for the prize of the high calling of God in Christ Jesus. Let us therefore, as many as be perfect, be thus minded: and if in anything ye be otherwise minded, God shall reveal even this unto you" Philippians 3:11,14,15.

It is to the benefit of the believer that the Cross makes a demand on his life. In the process of counting the cost, the believer, inevitably, gazes at the prize (Glory) - the glory of the Cross. The Price (Cost) and Prize are two sides of the same coin. Jesus considered them both when He was confronting the Cross, as recorded in Hebrews 12:2.

"Looking unto Jesus the author and finisher of our faith; who for the joy that was set before him endured the cross, despising the shame, and is set down at the right hand of the throne of God" Hebrews 12:2.

FOOTPRINTS FOR DISCIPLES

In confronting His Cross, Jesus left footprints for His disciples to follow Him. The footprints are fourfold, as recorded in Luke 9:23:

> 1. Come after Me,
>
> 2. Deny himself,
>
> 3. Take up his cross daily and
>
> 4. Follow Me.

"And He said to them all, if any man will come after Me, let him deny himself, and take up his cross daily, and follow Me" Luke 9:23.

Footprint #1: Come After Me

Coming to Jesus is the first step to counting the Cost. All who must count the cost of the Cross must first come to Him who bore the Cross for humanity. Jesus bore His Cross on behalf of mankind. We cannot come to the Cross outside of Jesus.

Every cross apart from the Cross of Christ is unacceptable to the Father. The scripture in Hebrews 12:2 captures it this way: "Looking unto Jesus the author and finisher of our faith". Jesus Christ is the Author and Finisher of our faith. We must look unto Him. We must take a cue from Him or put it another way, we must come to Him. Coming to Jesus is not only the first step but it is also the easiest part of the Pilgrim's Journey. All we do at this stage is to simple respond to His call.

"Come unto me, all ye that labour and are heavy laden, and I will give you rest" Matthew 11:28.

It is after we have come that we are confronted with the yoke of the LORD. We will discuss this in the last footprint: "Follow Me."

"Take my yoke upon you, and learn of me; for I am meek and lowly in heart: and ye shall find rest unto your souls. For my yoke is easy, and my burden is light" Matthew 11:29-30.

It is in coming to Jesus that we learn how to count the cost. He says, "learn of Me", implying discovery of new information and methodology of counting the cost. It is also in coming to Him that we learn from His example.

"For even hereunto were ye called: Because Christ also suffered for us, Leaving us an example, that ye should Follow His steps" 1 Peter 2:21.

Without the learning curve and the training of the LORD, the believer stops short of going to the next phase on the pilgrim's journey, which is "Deny Himself". That is why the LORD says emphatically, "many are called but few are chosen" (Matthew 22:14).

Footprint #2: Deny Himself

One who has come to Jesus needs to take the next step: Denying Himself. Between coming to Jesus and moving to the next step is the demand for absolute surrender. For without absolute surrender, coming to Jesus makes little or no profit. It is important to take this step early enough in the pilgrim's journey, otherwise the remainder of the steps would be difficult and near impossible. What does self-denial or deny himself really mean? Self-denial is simply death to self-will. A disciple of Christ must have no personal agenda; he exists only for the Master's agenda. The LORD knows that the self-life must be dealt with (crucified), otherwise the believer cannot be discipled along the way. We are in a way called to live a substituted life: We hand over our lives to Christ and Christ hands over His life to us. That is what Paul meant in Galatians 2:20 by the classic expression of "Yet not I, but Christ."

"I am crucified with Christ: nevertheless, I live; yet not I, but Christ liveth in me: and the life which I now live in the flesh I live by the faith of the Son of God, who loved me, and gave himself for me" Galatians 2:20. (Emphasis Mine)

In other scriptures (Ephesians 4:22-24, Colossians 3:9-10), Paul talks about the old man and the new man. The old man is the flesh or self-will and the new man is Jesus Christ or the Spirit of Christ (The Holy Spirit). The old life is substituted by the new life in Christ Jesus. It is this substituted life that moulds self-denial that the LORD requires of His disciples.

"That ye put off concerning the former conversation the old man, which is corrupt according to the deceitful lusts; And be renewed in the spirit of your mind; And that ye put on the new man, which after God is created in righteousness and true holiness" Ephesians 4:22-24.

Another way to describe self-denial through the substituted life is the giving up of the life of flesh for the life of the Spirit in Christ Jesus. When a man becomes born again (that is come to Jesus), he is confronted with the battle between the flesh and the spirit. Self or flesh is the enemy of spiritual life. It is the enemy within. The flesh (the old nature) still wants to call the shots but the spirit (the new nature) disputes with the old nature that Christ is now in charge. The battle is lost or won to the extent that the believer yields or fails to yield to the Spirit of Christ, according to the following scriptures"

"This I say then, Walk in the Spirit, and ye shall not fulfil the lust of the flesh. For the flesh lusteth against the Spirit, and the Spirit against the flesh: and these are contrary the one to the other: so that ye cannot do the things that ye would. But if ye be led of the Spirit, ye are not under the law" Galatians 5:16-18.

"Therefore we are buried with him by baptism into death: that like as Christ was raised up from the dead by the glory of the Father, even so we also should walk in newness of life...Neither yield ye your members as instruments of unrighteousness unto sin: but yield yourselves unto God, as those that are alive from the dead, and your members as instruments of righteousness unto God" Romans 6:4,13.

"For they that are after the flesh do mind the things of the flesh; but they that are after the Spirit the things of the Spirit" Romans 8:5.

Without the substituted life, the believer would simply fall through the crack of self or flesh life. Satan manipulates man to enthrone self-life in order to defeat the spirit life. The believer is often drawn or pulled one way or the other, but he must take a stance to live the substituted life daily. It is not a question of both lives but one life - one life in Christ.

"I protest by your rejoicing which I have in Christ Jesus our LORD, I die daily" 1 Corinthians 15:31.

Footprint #3: Take Up His Cross Daily

Having purposed to live the substituted life, the believer is now faced with what the LORD describes as "Take up his cross daily". No one can follow Jesus if he is not ready to take up his CROSS DAILY. Remember, the last step is "Follow Me". There is always a cross to confront if one must follow Jesus, the "Man of the Cross." What does it mean to "Take up his cross Daily?" Taking his cross daily means the willingness by the believer to endure hardship for the cause of Christ daily, even unto death. Living the substituted life attracts opposition from the host of hell, the world and even friends. The believer must therefore be ready to endure shame, hardship, sorrow, persecution or even pay the supreme price of death, rather than give up the substituted life.

> *"Thou therefore endure hardness, as a good soldier of Jesus Christ. No man that warreth entangleth himself with the affairs of this life; that he may please him who hath chosen him to be a soldier. And if a man also strive for masteries, yet is he not crowned, except he strive lawfully"* 2 Timothy 2:3-5.

The believer must come to the point of faith where he knows that life is more tragic than blissful for anyone who chooses to follow Jesus. Jesus did not promise us a trouble-free ride through life. He promises us safe arrival because of His finished work on the Cross.

> *"These things I have spoken unto you, that in me ye might have peace. In the world ye shall have tribulation: but be of good cheer; I have overcome the world" John 16:33.*

> *"Yea, and all that will live godly in Christ Jesus shall suffer persecution" 2 Timothy 3:12.*

The love of Christ for the believer is so strong that the trouble of this life cannot extinguish it. When a believer comes to terms with the depth, breath and height of the love of Christ for him, he would face any of life challenges with the blessed hope that the LORD will see him through whether in this life or the life to come.

> *"Who shall separate us from the love of Christ? shall tribulation, or distress, or persecution, or famine, or nakedness, or peril, or sword? As it is written, For thy sake we are killed all day long; we are accounted as sheep for the slaughter. Nay, in all these things we are more than conquerors through him that loved us. For I am persuaded, that neither death, nor life, nor angels, nor principalities, nor powers, nor things present, nor things to come, Nor height, nor depth, nor any other creature, shall be able to separate us from the love of God, which is in Christ Jesus our Lord" Romans 8:35-39.*

Footprint #4: And Follow Me

The last step in counting the Cost is "And Follow Me". Note the word "And" comes before "Follow Me". Jesus had listed the previous steps we have considered (Coming to Me, Deny Himself, Take up his cross daily) as pre-conditions for following Him, knowing that the natural disposition of a new believer would be to jump into the foray of followership without considering the challenges along the way which may actually takes him out of the way. This is because Jesus knows that following Him can only be made easy if those preconditions are firmly met. It is also a way of testing the seriousness and resilience of the new believer, knowing that "many are called but few are chosen".

> *"Take my yoke upon you, and learn of me; for I am meek and lowly in heart: and ye shall find rest unto your souls. For my yoke is easy, and my burden is light" Matthew 11:29-30.*

Coming to Jesus, denying himself, taking up his cross daily are simply the preparations of the heart, attitude and mind of the believer towards following Jesus. What then does it mean to "Follow Me"? Following involves taking Jesus' yoke and learning of Him. In this sense, following is the beginning of discipleship. It is as we follow that we become His disciple. Also, to follow Jesus, means, He is with us in every situation: we are yoked to Him. We are not apart or dismembered from Him. As we follow Him, we are sure to end the journey of faith well. Remember, Jesus is the author and finisher of our faith (Hebrews 12:2).

CHAPTER SIX

The Offence Of The Cross

Hymn: What a Friend We have in Jesus
1. What a Friend we have in Jesus,
All our sins and griefs to bear!
What a privilege to carry
Everything to God in prayer!
O what peace we often forfeit,
O what needless pain we bear,
All because we do not carry
Everything to God in prayer!

2. Have we trials and temptations?
Is there trouble anywhere?
We should never be discouraged,
Take it to the Lord in prayer.
Can we find a friend so faithful
Who will all our sorrows share?

Jesus knows our every weakness,
Take it to the Lord in prayer.

3. Are we weak and heavy-laden,
Cumbered with a load of care?
Precious Savior, still our refuge—
Take it to the Lord in prayer;
Do thy friends despise, forsake thee?
Take it to the Lord in prayer;
In His arms He'll take and shield thee,
Thou wilt find a solace there.

The Hymn, What a Friend We have in Jesus, is a clear reminder of the love Jesus Christ has for believers, even in tough times. The LORD grants us the privilege of taking every of life's issues to Him in prayer. No other faith matches the privilege of praying to a loving Saviour. It is in the light of this and many more reason that the world is offended by the simplicity and efficacy of the Christian faith. But the most offending part of the Christian faith to the world is the Cross of Christ.

Billy Graham in a sermon in 1958 had this to say on the issue of the offence of the Cross "I can preach anything else, and it's called popular. It pleases the ear, "But when I come to the heart of Christianity, when I come to the cross and the blood and the resurrection, that is the stumbling block. That's the thing people do not want to hear." This is true today as it was when Billy Graham spoke those words. It is to be observed today that the Church rather than take a stance for the preaching of the Cross of Christ, have capitulated, under pressure from the world (and sometimes from members), to the preaching of popular sermons. Who will save the offended Church?

The preaching of the Cross offends the world, satan and his evil agents. In fact, satan is so afraid of the Cross that he would do anything to stop the mere mention of the Cross of Christ. For it was at the Cross that his defeat was openly displayed (Colossians 2:15). And to the religious establishment and canal believers, the preaching of the Cross offends too. This is what Paul had to say on the matter:

> "For the Jews require a sign, and the Greeks seek after wisdom: But we preach Christ crucified, unto the Jews a stumbling block, and unto the Greeks foolishness; But unto them which are called, both Jews and Greeks, Christ the power of God, and the wisdom of God" 1 Corinthians 1:22-24.

The preaching of the Cross is a stumbling block and foolishness to people of other faith and the world in general. They just cannot believe the simplicity of the message of the Cross and the power to save therefrom. And, so what do they do? They get offended! We will explore in this Chapter, the meaning of the offence, reasons for the offence, manifestations of the offence and message to the offended.

Meaning Of The Offence Of The Cross

What does it mean to be offended? According to Pastor Craig Ledbetter in his sermon on the offence of the Cross, "it is to irritate, upset, annoy, disturb, insult, or make sick. Like the bad odour, blast of a car's horn behind you at a traffic light or yapping of a dog all night outside the window". People don't mind the preaching of the Jesus who does miracles or feeds the four thousand. When it comes to the Jesus who went to the cross, they get offended. The reasons are not far-fetched. The Cross makes demands on the world of lost sinners and the saints who have come to the saving grace of Jesus. Even the saints sometimes get offended by the Cross. Anytime Jesus spoke about His Cross to the disciples, they got offended (See Matthew 16:21-23; Matthew 26:31; John 6:24-27,60-62,66-67).

> "From that time forth began Jesus to shew unto his disciples, how that he must go unto Jerusalem, and suffer many things of the elders and chief priests and scribes, and be killed, and be raised again the third day. Then Peter took him, and began to rebuke him, saying, Be it far from thee, Lord: this shall not be unto thee. But he turned, and said unto Peter, Get thee behind me, Satan: thou art an offence unto me: for thou savourest not the things that be of God, but those that be of men" Matthew 16:21-23.

Isn't it strange that people don't get offended at any of the other faith like they do Christianity? What do you think is at the root of this offence? It is the Cross! The main stream media is very accommodating of the nuances of Islam, for example, despite the distasteful manifestations of the religion in our world today. They hardly get offended at suicide bombing. It is just another normal news headline today. In fact, the Mayor of London, Sadiq Khan, a muslin, once said that terrorism must be accepted as the new normal for big cities in the 21st Century. Isn't it strange that Londoners don't get offended at such doctrine? In the United States of America, the sign of the Cross is haunted by the Liberals, to take it out of public buildings, Churches and schools. Just the mere sign or replica of the Cross!

The Cross offends. But it only offends those who are perishing. That is the truth! To the one perishing, the Cross produces an odour of death but to the believer, it produces a fragrance of the Risen Christ. If the Cross offends anyone today, they should know that the remedy to that problem is in the Cross itself.

> *"Wherefore also it is contained in the scripture, Behold, I lay in Sion a chief corner stone, elect, precious: and he that believeth on him shall not be confounded. Unto you therefore which believe he is precious: but unto them which be disobedient, the stone which the builders disallowed, the same is made the head of the corner, And a stone of stumbling, and a rock of offence, even to them which stumble at the word, being disobedient: whereunto also they were appointed" 1 Peter 2:6-8.*

Paul came head on at the offence of the Cross and concluded that no matter what we do (whether we preach circumcision or not) the offence of the Cross has not ceased. But we need to understand the reasons for the offence, its manifestations and a message for the offended.

> *"But if I, brothers, still preach circumcision, why am I still being persecuted? In that case the offense of the cross has been removed" Galatians 5:11.*

The world's hatred is sometimes a sign that we are being faithful to Scripture, provided the world detests us due to the message we preach, not because we are obnoxious. Martin Luther said, "when the cross is abolished, and the rage of tyrants and heretics ceases on the one side, and all things are in peace, this is a sure token that the pure doctrine of God's Word is taken away." If we meet no worldly opposition, it may mean we are not being true to the offence of the cross.

Reasons For The Offence

What is it that offends people about the Cross? According to Pastor Graig Ledbetter, the reasons are not far-fetched and includes but not limited to the following:

The Cross Is Offensive Because Of Its Simplicity

The Cross is not complicated. The Cross gives access to eternal life (the resurrected life), what everyone wants but can't seem to find through drugs, medicine, meditation, etc! Man would rather prefer the rituals of the law to achieve eternal life. Man does not seem to appreciate that salvation by faith is adequate for the attainment of eternal life. But the Cross simply requires faith in Jesus Christ alone. People want some work of their hands to attain eternal life, but Jesus looks for faith from the heart, and people don't like to be told that something is wrong with their hearts!

So, man is offended at the thought of a dying saviour and a once-and-for-all sacrifice for atonement for sins. But Christ promises that only He can give eternal life - not dealing with physical life, but with the soul and spirit! But the life He offers requires His death as a sacrifice. Add anything else, and you complicate what God meant for a child to grasp (Matthew 18:1-4).

The Cross Is Offensive Because Of Its Conclusions

The Cross has concluded us ALL under sin, and therefore, ALL will die (Romans 6:23). The Cross has concluded that ALL need Christ - no exceptions, no other Saviour, and no matter how good we are (Isaiah 64:6; Acts 4:12). People don't like those kind of "judgmental" statements. They want a religious system that tells them they are OK! They get offended at a Holy God who is revolted by our sin! But it's true! That's why people would rather read books ABOUT the Bible, than read it for themselves, because they don't like its approach to the Human race - lost, on its way to hell and in need of a Saviour!

The Cross Is Offensive Because Of Its Sacrifice

The Cross is not a picnic - It was a bloody, violent judgment for the sins of the whole world, placed upon One Person, all on the Cross! Christ was on the Cross dealing with a substitution of His life for ours. He was dealing with a bloody sacrifice (Hebrews 10:5,10-12) for our sins. People don't want to confront their sins this way. They prefer to make excuses like Adam (Genesis 3:12) or cover up their sins (Genesis 3:8) or simply wish it away (Genesis 3:6). But God has always intended the judgment of sin to be an open court session. He sacrificed His Son on the hills of Calvary, for all eyes to see. Man doesn't want an open court and so he rejects the Cross for exposing his sins and judging it openly by the death of Jesus Christ.

The Cross Is Offensive Because Of Man's Pride

The people at the foot of the Cross were offended and began to wag their tongues against Jesus, the same Jesus who they once hailed but now were chanting 'crucify him'. In the crowd, everyone wanted to give the impression that the problem was with Jesus, not with themselves - how convenient - blame the teacher! But the problem was not with Jesus - they just didn't want to find out the answer.

"And they that passed by reviled him, wagging their heads, And saying, Thou that destroyest the temple, and buildest it in three days, save thyself. If thou be the Son of God, come down from the cross. Likewise also the chief

priests mocking him, with the scribes and elders, said, He saved others; himself he cannot save. If he be the King of Israel, let him now come down from the cross, and we will believe him. He trusted in God; let him deliver him now, if he will have him: for he said, I am the Son of God. The thieves also, which were crucified with him, cast the same in his teeth" Matthew 27:39-44.

People are too proud to think for ourselves - always want to let someone else do the thinking for them. They want someone to "interpret" life (fortune tellers, palm readers, tarot cards); to interpret the Bible (priests, bishops, catechisms, missals). So Jesus confounds, or confuses these people on purpose (1 Corinthians 1:27-29) and sets up a stumbling block! He has to, or else they would just keep pretending that they are following Him, when they are only following the miracles, excitement, good times, free food, and good company!

The Cross Is Offensive Because Of Its Challenge

People want a Bible that is easy and does not "rub them the wrong way" (2 Timothy 4:2-4). No athlete would waste 5 minutes with a coach who did not push them, challenge them, and urge them on farther! The damnation of this world is found in its complacency, and religious smugness! The Cross tests our desire to know the truth - to get the answers. It tests our commitment - even when we don't fully understand the LORD, and when He is not popular! Are we committed to paying the price or counting the cost?

The Cross Is Offensive Because It Nullifies The Ordinances Of The Law

The Cross is the end of the law and its demands for righteousness. The Jews could not comprehend why the Cross should replace the law, the ordinances and the tradition of the elders. Paul had a hectic time convincing the Jews of the invincibility of the Cross and was persecuted for daring to challenge the established order with the doctrine of the Cross.

> *"For they being ignorant of God's righteousness, and going about to establish their own righteousness, have not submitted themselves unto the righteousness of God. For Christ is the end of the law for righteousness to everyone that believeth" Romans 10:3-4.* (Emphasis Mine)

> *"Blotting out the handwriting of ordinances that was against us, which was contrary to us, and took it out of the way, nailing it to his cross" Colossians 2:14.*

> *"For in Jesus Christ neither circumcision availeth anything, nor uncircumcision; but faith which worketh by love.... And I, brethren, if I yet preach circumcision, why do I yet suffer persecution? Then is the offence of the cross ceased" Galatians 5:6, 11.*

The Cross has ended such ordinances, rules, rituals, liturgies and practices as new moon, sabbath, animal sacrifices, ceremonials, feasts (unleavened bread, harvest, first fruits, weeks, Passover), temple worship, feet washing, the Levitical order, etc.

> *"But now, after that ye have known God, or rather are known of God, how turn ye again to the weak and beggarly elements, whereunto ye desire again to be in bondage? Ye observe days, and months, and times, and years. I am afraid of you, lest I have bestowed upon you labour in vain" Galatians 4:9-11.*

This offends the Jews and even today's Church which is bent on practicing a medley of the Old and New Covenants but what says the scriptures on such?

> *"For if that first covenant had been faultless, then should no place have been sought for the second. For finding fault with them, he saith, Behold, the days come, saith the Lord, when I will make a new covenant with the house of Israel and with the house of Judah:.. In that he saith, A new covenant, he hath made the first old. Now that which decayeth and waxeth old is ready to vanish away" Hebrews 8:7-8, 13.*

MANIFESTATION OF THE OFFENCE

Mocking Of The Faith

The Cross, from its inception, attracted disdain and disparagement from the people that witnessed it. We are told from scriptures that the priests, passers-by, the crowd and people mocked and wagged their tongues at the LORD of glory while hanging on the Cross. Some made disparaging statements, as follows:

"Likewise also the chief priests mocking him, with the scribes and elders, said, He saved others; himself he cannot save. If he be the King of Israel, let him now come down from the cross, and we will believe him. He trusted in God; let him deliver him now, if he will have him: for he said, I am the Son of God" Matthew 27:41-43.

"And they that passed by reviled him, wagging their heads, And saying, Thou that destroyest the temple, and buildest it in three days, save thyself. If thou be the Son of God, come down from the cross" Matthew 27:39-40.

Today, it comes by means of jeers, scoffs, shrug of the shoulder, and slanders. The mainstream media and liberals made caricatures of our faith in their commentaries and express a world view that is anti-Christianity. All these are the manifestations of the offence of the Cross.

Cruel Treatment Of Christians

In olden times, they did it by burning, torturing, and tormenting Christians, making them suffer all kinds of indescribable agonies. In many parts of the world today Christians are not just hated but haunted for their faith in the mainstream media, college campuses and courts in places like the Middle East, India, Indonesia, Europe and even the United States of America. Today, there is a resurgence of cruel treatment of Christians. We witnessed the Islamic State (ISIS) burned, crucified and beheaded Christians with the world standing by, for ISIS served their purpose: the offence of the Cross.

Persecution

Christians over the ages have suffered persecutions of varying degrees for their faith. The LORD had warned that persecution would come to His disciples because of their faith in Him. These have come in the form of private and open persecutions. The "offence of the cross" shows itself, sometimes, by private persecution. Every now and then, drunken husbands persecute their wives almost incessantly because they cleave fast to God! New believers often suffer persecution from their father and mother and sister and brother, for Christ's sake.

In extreme cases, persecutions are open. This comes in the form of hostility, imprisonment, loss of civic rights and property. The right to worship is severely curtailed in many parts of the world, most especially in countries or places with Muslim majority. The Middle East is offended by the Cross that most countries there criminalise the Christian faith and openly forbid Muslims from conversion to Christianity. They legislate against the Christian faith through the Anti-Conversion laws.

Wrong Doctrines

There is a subtle offence of the Cross in the way apostate churches adopts doctrines that are contrary to the work of the Cross. They circumvent the truth by parallel beliefs that have no scriptural foundations. Have you ever thought of how the so called "harmless" doctrines like infant baptism, wearing of plastic cross, celebration of Easter, Lent, Palm Sunday, Christmas, rituals, purgatory and Church tradition conspire to make the Cross of no effect? Just because they cannot stand the Cross, they invent their own. They end up with what the Bible calls 'form of godliness'.

> "Having a form of godliness, but denying the power thereof: from such turn away" 2 Timothy 3:5.

Death

The ultimate manifestation of the offence of the Cross is the risk of losing one's life for daring to trust the Crucified LORD. Believers over the age have accepted death instead of denying the Cross.

> "When they heard these things, they were cut to the heart, and they gnashed on him with their teeth... Then they cried out with a loud voice, and stopped their ears, and ran upon him with one accord, And cast him out of the city, and stoned him: and the witnesses laid down their clothes at a young man's feet, whose name was Saul" Acts 7:54, 57-59.

"Now about that time Herod the king stretched forth his hands to vex certain of the church. And he killed James the brother of John with the sword. And because he saw it pleased the Jews, he proceeded further to take Peter also. (Then were the days of unleavened bread.) And when he had apprehended him, he put him in prison, and delivered him to four quaternions of soldiers to keep him; intending after Easter to bring him forth to the people" Acts 12:1-4.

Message To The Offended

History has taught us that it is counter-productive to kick against the Cross. The Jews tried it and failed. The Romans tried it and failed. The Catholic Church tried unsuccessfully, and many more attempts have faltered and only succeeded in displaying the foolishness of man. It is foolish to be offended at the cross, seeing that no man can stop its progress! Opposing the Cross is like standing in front of an approaching underground train, with no escape route. C.H. Spurgeon, had this to say in a Sermon he delivered as far back as 1856:

"Who are you to attempt to stand against it? You will be crushed; but let me tell you that, when the car goes over you, the wheel will not be raised even an inch by your size. For what are you? A tiny gnat, a creeping worm, which that wheel will crush to less than nothing, and not leave you even a name as having been an opponent of the gospel. There have been men who have stood up, and said, "We will stop the chariot of Christ." Thousands have looked at them and have been afraid. Their trumpets have blown loud and long, and some poor Christians have said, "Stand aside! Here comes a man who will stop the chariot of the Lord Jesus." At one time, it was Tom Paine; then it was Robert Owen; but what became of them? Did the chariot stop for them? No; it went on just as if there had never been a Tom Paine or a Robert Owen on the earth. Let all the infidels in the world know assuredly that the gospel will win its way, whatever they may do. Poor creatures! Their efforts to oppose it are not worthy of our notice; and we need not fear that they can stop the truth. As well might a gnat think to quench the sun. Go, tiny insect, and do it, if you can. You will only burn your wings and die. As well might a fly think it could drink the ocean dry. Drink the ocean, if you can; more likely, you will sink in it, and so it will drink you. You who despise and oppose the gospel; what can you do? It comes on "conquering and to conquer." I always think that, the more enemies the gospel has, the more it will advance...O man! If you hate the gospel, let me say to you solemnly how doubly foolish you are to be offended with Christ, who is the only One who can save you! As well might the drowning man be offended with the rope which is cast to him, and which is the only means of his escape; as well might the dying patient be offended with the cup of medicine which is put to his lips, and which alone can save his body from death; as well might the man whose house is burning be offended with the fireman who roughly puts the fire escape ladder against his window—as that you should be offended with Christ. Offended with Him who would snatch you as "a brand from the burning"? Offended with Him who alone can quench for you the fire of hell? Offended with Him whose blood alone can wash you white, and give you a place with Him in glory everlasting? Offended with Him? Then you are mad indeed. Not Bedlam itself can produce a maniac more foolish than you are. Ah, you despisers, you shall wonder and perish! You are offended with the gospel because it says that you have not any merit; but you have not any, then why are you offended? You are offended at the gospel because it does not ask anything of you in order that you may be saved; yet, if it did demand anything of you as a condition of your salvation, you would be lost. It is just the gospel for you; it is made on purpose; it fits your condition; it is adapted to your case—and yet you are offended with it! Oh, how can you be so foolish? Did you ever hear of a man who was offended with a coach that was carrying him, because it had wheels? Why should you be offended with the gospel chariot because it could not advance except on the wheels of free grace? What! You are offended with the gospel because it lays you low? Don't you know that it is the very best place for you? The devil would have you very high if he could; but that would be only that he might ruin you."

"My dear friends, I beseech you, in the name of the Lord Jesus Christ Himself, do think why you are offended with the gospel. I know it goes against your prejudices; when you first hear it, you do not love it; but, remember, it is your only hope of salvation. Are you offended with that which alone can save you? Offended with that which can put a crown on your head, a palm branch in your hand, and give you bliss forever? Then, I think, when you sink to hell, you will look up to heaven, and say, "Ah, Christ! I was offended with You, and now I see that You are the only Savior. I hated Your name, of which it is written, 'At the name of Jesus, every knee shall bow.' I hated that Savior who was the only Savior to redeem sinners from sin."

Saul (who later became Paul, the Apostle) was so offended by the Cross that he persecuted Christians, supervised the death of Stephen and others. But he met his waterloo on the way to Damascus where he went to compel the religious establishment there to hand over Christians to be punished in Jerusalem. This is what the LORD said to him on the road to Damascus.

> *"And as he journeyed, he came near Damascus: and suddenly there shined round about him a light from heaven: And he fell to the earth, and heard a voice saying unto him, Saul, Saul, why persecutest thou me? And he said, Who art thou, Lord? And the Lord said, I am Jesus whom thou persecutest: it is hard for thee to kick against the pricks. And he trembling and astonished said, Lord, what wilt thou have me to do? And the Lord said unto him, Arise, and go into the city, and it shall be told thee what thou must do" Acts 9:3-6.*

The message to the offended, therefore, is that "it is hard for you to kick against the pricks." Paul got the message and took the right steps to become a Christian. And so, should every offended today. Otherwise it is a blatant waste of time to fight the Cross. The Cross is eternal and works for the benefits of the fallen man. It is God's gift to a world of lost sinners. It cost Jesus everything and so it is too priceless to miss and too expensive to attempt to fight. If the Cross offends anyone today, they should know that the remedy to that problem is in the Cross itself.

At The Foot Of The Cross

CHAPTER SEVEN

The Eternal Cross

Hymn: Rock of Ages

1. Rock of Ages, cleft for me,
Let me hide myself in Thee;
Let the water and the blood,
From Thy riven side which flowed,
Be of sin the double cure,
Save me from its guilt and power.

2. Not the labor of my hands
Can fulfill Thy law's demands;
Could my zeal no respite know,
Could my tears forever flow,
All could never sin erase,
Thou must save, and save by grace.

3. Nothing in my hands I bring,
Simply to Thy cross I cling;

Naked, come to Thee for dress,
Helpless, look to Thee for grace:
Foul, I to the fountain fly,
Wash me, Savior, or I die.

4. While I draw this fleeting breath,
When mine eyes shall close in death,
When I soar to worlds unknown,
See Thee on Thy judgment throne,
Rock of Ages, cleft for me,
Let me hide myself in Thee.

The Hymn: "Rock of Ages", pictures the Crucified Christ as the Rock that meets the need of all over the ages. He meets these needs   before, during and after life. The Hymn is a picture of the Eternal Cross. In Chapter One, a call to the Cross of Christ was discussed. We ex-rayed the two scenes of the Cross, as seen by eye witnesses and the later days believers. In addition to believing in the Cross to the saving of our souls, we are required to behold the Cross as eternal. Beholding the eternal Cross is the ultimate scene of the events of the Cross as it enables us to go into the mind of God from eternity past, present and eternity future. Beholding the eternal Cross is the most profuse and profound scene.

Having come to the Cross, we cannot abandon it in our work of faith here on earth and beyond time. We can safely conclude that the Cross is more than an historical event. It is an eternal event. It has provisions for the Old Testament Saints who looked forward to the coming of the Messiah, the eye witnesses and all believers to the end of the age. In this Chapter we will examine the Cross in the Eternity Past, Eternity Present and Eternity Future.

The Cross in the Eternity Past (From the Dateless Past to Old Testament Dispensation)

The Cross has been in the mind of God from the time the foundation of the world was laid. Redemption was no last-minute thought, brought into being to meet an emergency. No sooner had sin entered the garden than God spoke of One who was to come and who was to bruise the serpent's (that is, Satan's) head, His own heel being bruised in the process (Genesis 3:15), and to restore all the damage which sin and satan had done. God thereby revealed that the sad turn of events had not taken Him by surprise, but that there was One in reserve to meet this very situation (Roy and Revel Hession, 1950). Revelations 13:8 calls Him (that is, Jesus), "the Lamb slain from the foundation of the world". Jesus was slain eternally and what happened at Calvary was an enactment of that which already had been. Thus, the remedy for the sin question antedated the disease.

The Old Testament is full of the shadow narratives of the Cross of Christ. We examine hereunder a few of them:

"And I will put enmity between thee and the woman, and between thy seed and her seed; it shall bruise thy head, and thou shalt bruise his heel" Genesis 3:15.

The above Scripture gives a glimpse of the Cross as God's triumph card in responding immediately to the tragedy of sin brought upon mankind by Adam and Eve in the Garden of Eden. It shows that God was not taken by surprise. The solution was ready-made and not an after-thought. He didn't need to wait to examine options. Of course, there were no options. The Cross has no alternatives. It is sufficient in purpose and scope. God went a little further to herald the Cross by clothing Adam and Eve with animal skin from a slain animal to foreshadow the need for blood for the remission of sin. Remember, Adam's post sin spiritual condition was akin to nakedness, as every sinner since then is, and God symbolic remedy was skin coat from a slain animal, immediately shedding blood to give them a cover.

Another herald of the Cross of Christ was the symbolic offering of Abraham's only son, Isaac, in obedience to God.

"And he said, Take now thy son, thine only son Isaac, whom thou lovest, and get thee into the land of Moriah; and offer him there for a burnt offering upon one of the mountains which I will tell thee of" Genesis 22:2.

This foreshadows God's offering of His only begotten Son, Jesus, incidentally at the same site (known as Moriah in Old Testament and Golgotha in the New Testament) where Abraham was to sacrifice Isaac. Isaac was laid on the wood (foreshadow of the wooden cross); Isaac carried the wood the same way Jesus bore His Cross to Golgotha; God provided a lamb for the sacrifice and Jesus is known severally in the Scripture as the Lamb of God. Abraham stretched out his hands to slay his son, Isaac the same way God, the Father superintended over the sacrifice of His Son, Jesus at Calvary.

> *"But he was wounded for our transgressions, he was bruised for our iniquities: the chastisement of our peace was upon him; and with his stripes we are healed…He was oppressed, and he was afflicted, yet he opened not his mouth: he is brought as a lamb to the slaughter, and as a sheep before her shearers is dumb, so he openeth not his mouth.…Yet it pleased the LORD to bruise him; he hath put him to grief: when thou shalt make his soul an offering for sin, he shall see his seed, he shall prolong his days, and the pleasure of the LORD shall prosper in his hand. He shall see of the travail of his soul, and shall be satisfied: by his knowledge shall my righteous servant justify many; for he shall bear their iniquities" Isaiah 53:5, 7, 10-11.*

Prophet Isaiah had the rare insight into the window of eternity past to preview the sacrificial offering of God's Son, Jesus Christ, the Messiah for the remission of sins. And

Isaiah 53 above is a compendium of the travail of the LORD on the Cross. We have referenced verses 5, 7, 10-11 above to picture the Cross in the eternity past. Prophet Isaiah foretold of the suffering of the LORD in very graphic terms, including he was wounded for our transgressions, he was bruised for our iniquities, ...he is brought as a lamb to the slaughter, Yet it pleased the LORD to bruise him; he hath put him to grief: when thou shalt make his soul an offering for sin. This is the picture of God's mind regarding the Cross of Christ. Jesus went to the Cross as a Sacrificial Lamb; He was wounded and bruised; God was pleased with His offering for sin.

The import of this phase of the Cross is that the proceeds of the Cross was extended to the Old Testament saints who hoped on the coming of the Messiah as foretold by the prophets, the law and scriptures. If it were not so, they would have lost out. For these and many other reasons, it became necessary for the Cross to be eternal, covering past, present and future dispensations. Many of the Old Testament saints suffered persecutions of the Eternal Cross and yet held on hoping for a time when the physical Cross would be made manifest to the nation of Israel and the whole world, thereafter. They were encouraged by various Messianic Prophecies and Psalms. We chronicled the Messianic Psalms and Prophecies in my book, The Three Silent Days and Nights, pages 39-49.

Hebrews chapter 11, commonly known as "the hall of faith", pictures the generation of the Old Testament saints who hoped on the coming of the Messiah for their redemption. We produce hereunder snippets of the references to their faith from Hebrews 11.

> *"These all died in faith, not having received the promises, but having seen them afar off, and were persuaded of them, and embraced them, and confessed that they were strangers and pilgrims on the earth" Hebrews 11:13.* (Emphasis Mine)

> *"By faith Moses, when he was come to years, refused to be called the son of Pharaoh's daughter; Choosing rather to suffer affliction with the people of God, than to enjoy the pleasures of sin for a season; Esteeming the reproach of Christ greater riches than the treasures in Egypt: for he had respect unto the recompence of the reward. By faith he forsook Egypt, not fearing the wrath of the king: for he endured, as seeing him who is invisible" Hebrews 11:24-27.* (Emphasis Mine)

> *"Women received their dead raised to life again: and others were tortured, not accepting deliverance; that they might obtain a better resurrection" Hebrews 11:35.* (Emphasis Mine)

"And these all, having obtained a good report through faith, received not the promise: God having provided some better thing for us, that they without us should not be made perfect" Hebrews 11:39-40. (Emphasis Mine)

Note the phrases highlights in the above referenced verses from Hebrews 11 all points to the Cross of Christ which formed the basis for the hope of the Old Testament saints. They saw the Cross afar off (meaning it was to happen in the future, that is in the New Testament dispensation). Moses esteemed the reproach of Christ (the Cross) far better than the sinful pleasures of living in the palace as Pharaoh's daughter's son. He led the Israelites out of bondage from Egypt, as a prefiguration of Jesus offering redemption to mankind out of the world of lost sinners. He did all these, having seen in the spirit the invisible Messiah at that time. Those Old Testament saints put their hope in the resurrection to be offered by the Risen Christ and so were not mindful of the temporary sufferings they had to go through in the hands of their tormentors. Above all, God had reserved the physical manifestation of the Cross for the New Testament dispensation, not wanting the Old Testament Saints to lose out but also to bring them alongside the New Testament saints. This is eloquently captured in Hebrews 11:39-40 as "And these all, having obtained a good report through faith, received not the promise: God having provided some better thing for us, that they without us should not be made perfect. Glory to God, the Father, for His unfathomable wisdom, love and plan for man!

The Cross in the Eternity Present (From the New Testament Dispensation to End of Time)

In this phase, the Cross was actualised on earth at a specific place (Golgotha) and time. The physical Cross was enacted as a basis for those who were not part of the history to believe through the preaching of the Gospel. The Cross was made real to man in this dispensation. Peter profusely and profoundly portrayed the eternal cross by linking the Old Testament prophecies to the events of the Cross at Golgotha at his famous Pentecost preaching in Acts 2. Here are excerpts from the sermon at Pentecost:

> *"Ye men of Israel, hear these words; Jesus of Nazareth, a man approved of God among you by miracles and wonders and signs, which God did by him in the midst of you, as ye yourselves also know: Him, being delivered by the determinate counsel and foreknowledge of God, ye have taken, and by wicked hands have crucified and slain: Whom God hath raised up, having loosed the pains of death: because it was not possible that he should be holden of it" Acts 2:22-24.*

> *"Therefore being a prophet, and knowing that God had sworn with an oath to him, that of the fruit of his loins, according to the flesh, he would raise up Christ to sit on his throne; He seeing this before spake of the resurrection*

of Christ, that his soul was not left in hell, neither his flesh did see corruption. This Jesus hath God raised up, whereof we all are witnesses" Acts 2:30-32.

"Therefore let all the house of Israel know assuredly, that God hath made that same Jesus, whom ye have crucified, both Lord and Christ" Acts 2:36.

Another exposition on the eternal Cross was offered by Apostle Paul, who more than any other person in his time, had deep understanding of the eternal cross. He persuaded both the Jews and Gentiles to accept the Cross as the only pathway to the salvation of man. Paul embraced fully the events of the Cross and made it the cornerstone of his faith in the Lord Jesus Christ and preaching to others.

"I am crucified with Christ: nevertheless I live; yet not I, but Christ liveth in me: and the life which I now live in the flesh I live by the faith of the Son of God, who loved me, and gave himself for me" Galatians 2:20.

"But God forbid that I should glory, save in the cross of our Lord Jesus Christ, by whom the world is crucified unto me, and I unto the world" Galatians 6:14.

"And Paul, as his manner was, went in unto them, and three sabbath days reasoned with them out of the scrip-

tures, Opening and alleging, that Christ must needs have suffered, and risen again from the dead; and that this Jesus, whom I preach unto you, is Christ" Acts 17:2-3.

The fact that the Cross of Christ still saves sinners today, two thousand years after, means that the Cross is more than a historical event. It is an eternal contract between God and man. The finished work on the Cross still works miracles today and brings immense benefits to mankind. This could not have been possible if the Cross was historical. Jesus said:

"And I, if I be lifted up from the earth, will draw all men unto me" John 12:32.

Here, Jesus was referring to the Cross ("If I be lifted up"), being able to draw men to God. People are persuaded by the Cross not because of its history but because of its eternal timeless solution to their need for salvation. The Cross has been preached and believed for over two thousand years because it is timeless and beyond time.

"Be it known unto you all, and to all the people of Israel, that by the name of Jesus Christ of Nazareth, whom ye crucified, whom God raised from the dead, even by him doth this man stand here before you whole" Acts 4:10.

The Cross in the Eternity Future (After the End of Time)

The first person who had the rare opportunity of touching the imprints of the Cross was Thomas, called Didymus. He was not around when Jesus appeared to the disciples after his resurrection. When he was told that the Lord had risen, he made a demand to see the print of the nails. How could he expect to see the print of the nails in a resurrected body? After all the new body should not carry anything from the old body. God allowed this for the eternal Cross to be revealed.

> *"The other disciples therefore said unto him, We have seen the Lord. But he said unto them, Except I shall see in his hands the print of the nails, and put my finger into the print of the nails, and thrust my hand into his side, I will not believe" John 20:25.*

Thomas was seeking the eternal Cross. Eight days later, Jesus offered Thomas the rare privilege of beholding the eternal Cross from the prints of the nails on His resurrected body.

> *"Then saith he to Thomas, Reach hither thy finger, and behold my hands; and reach hither thy hand, and thrust it into my side: and be not faithless, but believing" John 20:27.*

The scene of the eternal Cross (the imprints of the nails on Jesus hands and that of the piercing on His side from the sword of the Roman soldier) melted the doubt in the heart of Thomas and led to a positive confession.

> *"And Thomas answered and said unto him, My Lord and my God" John 20:28.*

The Cross has been in the mind of God from the time the foundation of the world was laid. That is why Jesus is described in Revelation 13:8 as "the Lamb slain from the foundation of the world". Jesus was slain eternally and what happened at Calvary was an enactment of that which already had been. Jesus is coming back, and every eye shall see Him. All the earth shall wail because of Him. Why? When they remember the Cross!

This is how Revelation 1:7 captures it: "…and they also which pierced him", a direct reference to the Cross. This is because the Cross is eternal, and time cannot obliterate it. This is not a reference to eyewitnesses of the physical Cross but all of humanity that caused the LORD to go to the Cross. In fact, Revelation 1:7 can be cross-referenced to the Old Testament account of the event of the eternal Cross in Zechariah 12:10.

> *"Behold, he cometh with clouds; and every eye shall see him, and they also which pierced him: and all kindreds of the earth shall wail because of him. Even so, Amen" Revelation 1:7.* (Emphasis Mine)

"And I will pour upon the house of David, and upon the inhabitants of Jerusalem, the spirit of grace and of supplications: and they shall look upon me whom they have pierced, and they shall mourn for him, as one mourneth for his only son, and shall be in bitterness for him, as one that is in bitterness for his firstborn" Zechariah 12:10. (Emphasis Mine)

When Jesus appeared to John in Revelations 1:18, He introduced Himself as "I AM he that liveth, and was dead; and behold I AM alive for evermore, Amen; and have the keys of hell and of death". This is a clear reference to the eternal Cross. This is a post-resurrection event, that took place many years after the physical Cross. And the LORD looked back at the Cross for His introduction. Again, we see here that the Cross has been the central theme of the dateless past, the present and will be forever. The LORD will forever bear the marks of the Cross, its emblem, title and narrative, such as the Lamb. Any reference to the LORD as a Lamb in eternity future portends the eternal Cross.

"And I beheld, and, lo, in the midst of the throne and of the four beasts, and in the midst of the elders, stood a Lamb as it had been slain, having seven horns and seven eyes, which are the seven Spirits of God sent forth into all the earth" Revelation 5:6. (Emphasis Mine)

Saying with a loud voice, Worthy is the Lamb that was slain to receive power, and riches, and wisdom, and strength, and honour, and glory, and blessing. And every creature which is in heaven, and on the earth, and under the earth, and such as are in the sea, and all that are in them, heard I saying, Blessing, and honour, and glory, and power, be unto him that sitteth upon the throne, and unto the Lamb for ever and ever" Revelation 5:12-13. (Emphasis Mine)

> *"Let us be glad and rejoice, and give honour to him: for the marriage of the Lamb is come, and his wife hath made herself ready" Revelation 19:7.*(Emphasis Mine)

> *"And I saw no temple therein: for the Lord God Almighty and the Lamb are the temple of it" Revelation 21:22.* (Emphasis Mine)

> *"And the city had no need of the sun, neither of the moon, to shine in it: for the glory of God did lighten it, and the Lamb is the light thereof" Revelation 21:23.* (Emphasis Mine)

Indeed, the Bible ends with references to the Lamb and the roles the LORD Jesus Christ will play in that capacity as conveyed on Him by the eternal Cross.

"And he shewed me a pure river of water of life, clear as crystal, proceeding out of the throne of God and of the Lamb" Revelation 22:1. (Emphasis Mine)

"And there shall be no more curse: but the throne of God and of the Lamb shall be in it; and his servants shall serve him" Revelation 22:3. (Emphasis Mine)

For the above and many more reasons, we are all called today to not only believe but also to behold the Cross as eternal and not as a mere historic occurrence. Jesus will forever carry the imprints of the Cross in His resurrected body as a memorial. The Saints in eternity future will behold the Cross as a memorial of the blessedness of the sacrificial offering of Jesus on the Cross, culminating in their eternal redemption. This will elicit eternal thanksgiving by the Saints of all ages and for all of eternity. We end our exposition on the Eternal Cross with the songs, "Behold the Lamb" and "All Heaven declares", as presented below:

Song: Behold the Lamb
Behold the Lamb
That was slain at Calvary (2 times)
I have victory through the Lamb
That was slain at Calvary (2 times)

Song: All Heaven Declares
1. All heaven declares
The glory of the risen Lord

Who can compare with
The beauty of the Lord

Refrain:
Forever He will be
The Lamb upon the throne
I gladly bow the knee
And worship Him alone

2. I will proclaim
The glory of the risen Lord
Who once was slain
To reconcile man to God

Refrain:
Forever You will be
The Lamb upon the throne
I gladly bow the knee
And worship You alone

One day, we will join the Saints in Heaven to sing along the isle of eternity to extol the LORD for the proceeds of the Cross, indeed, the Eternal Cross. Amen!

CHAPTER EIGHT

The Ultimate Decision

Dear friends, life is a bundle of choices. The choice we make today determines who and where we will be tomorrow. What we are today is the result of our choices made yesterday. The Almighty God gave us the right to choose: He gave us the free will, power and a conscience. But the LORD expects that we will first choose to follow Him as the foundation to making the other choices in life.

That is why He sent Jesus Christ to show us the way. Jesus and the finished work on the Cross is the central theme of this book. We have shown in this book how relevant the Cross of Christ is to the need of man for redemption. The Cross is eternal and would forever serve the best interest of man in eternity, as it has done in time.

Now I offer you the ultimate choice: choose now to walk with God or to be driven away from Him if you continue in your rebellion. He is asking you now, "What does it profit you to gain the whole world and lose your soul?" Of what use is life if the Author of Life is a missing coin in that life? I counsel that you choose to walk with Him. This do, by inviting Jesus Christ into your life for the Bible says "whosoever shall call on the name of the LORD shall be saved" - Acts 2:21. All these start, when you pray as follows:

"Dear Jesus, I believe that you died for me and rose again on the third day. I confess to you that I am a sinner. I need your forgiveness. Come into my life, forgive my sins and give me eternal life. Baptise me in the Holy Spirit. I confess that you are now my LORD. Thank you for my salvation. I walk in your peace and joy from this day forward. Amen".

Name...

Signature ....

Date..

Please email me via HYPERLINK "mailto:imoabasi@yahoo.com" imoabasi@yahoo.com and I will pray for you, thanking God for the choice you have made today.

Other Books By Imo-Abasi Jacob, Snr

Having read this book, *At the Foot of the Cross,* written with great passion and candour, I am persuaded that, the simplicity, the attractiveness, the sufficiency, and the glory of the Cross of Christ have impacted your life immensely. The Cross is intended to be at the center of everything we do in life, as profoundly expressed by the author.

Imo-Abasi Jacob, Snr, who is a teacher, a business coach, a regular resource person on leadership, business, biblical management principles and marketplace ethics, has authored the following books with the same candour and revelation, addressing different areas of life. You have the privilege to get copies of his books for yourself, friends and family.

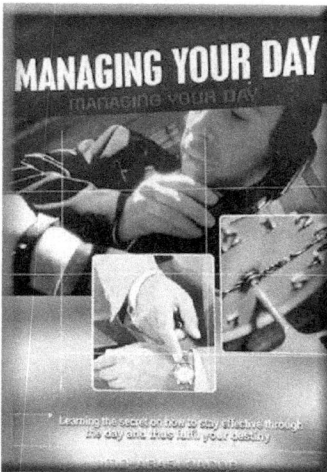

Managing Your Day provides insights into the proper use of time to fulfill destiny. It is a paradigm shift from the regular teachings on time management by business scholars. This book weaves the spiritual and physical perspectives of time and celebrates the best practice of Jesus on the use of time. It is only in this book that you will find the link between life and time. The book concludes that time wasted is life wasted and invites readers to carefully consider time saving strategies in their daily life routine.

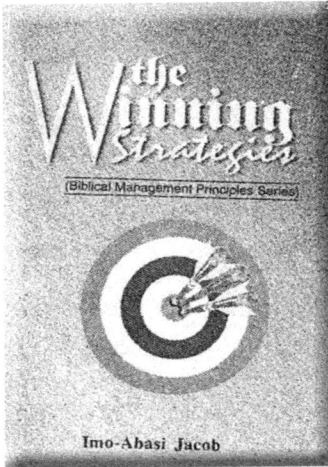

This book, "The Winning Strategies" is an answer to the prayer for the key to success in business. The financial turmoil in the global economy has had a traumatising effect on business owners. The insights in the book are meant to turn the tide around and launch the reader on the path of true prosperity needed to actualise the Great Commission. By reading this book, the word "winning" will take a new meaning to spur you to become a true regent of God on earth.

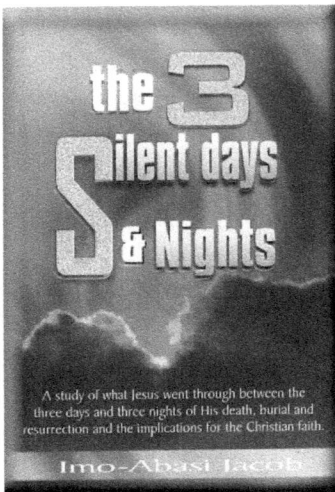

This book is God's answer to the author's quest for why the early Christians were more fervent than our generation. The Cross was their motivation. Our generation has drifted away from the Cross and embrace forms of godliness and religion. This book is a detour to the Cross, examining the events at the Cross and after the Cross in the three silent days and nights that Jesus was in the grave. It offers exciting revelations that can prepare our hearts once again for the Lord and His imminent return.

116

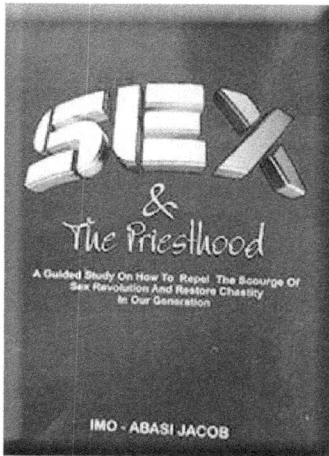

The topic of sex is one less talked about in the Christian community. The world is often the one to raise the advocacy, many times to the confusion of believers. It is the pop stars, the fashion designers, gay activists and New Agers that seem to be talking. This book is born out of the "hard talk" series of the author and is meant to draw the Church out of her comfort zone of silence on such an important topic like sex. It is also meant to expose the sin of sexual immorality in the Church and reposition believers for their priestly functions.

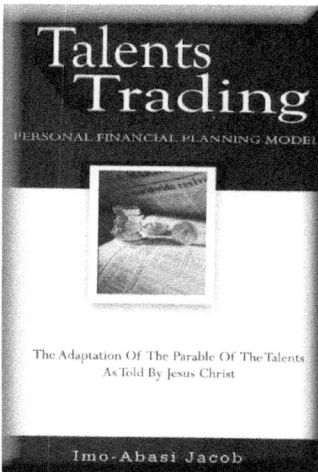

Talents Trading is an answer to the question on why some people are poor, and others are rich. The Parable of Talents confirms God's desire for all to have financial productivity to showcase His Kingdom here on earth. It shows how to achieve financial productivity and fulfill destiny in God. You will find the simplicity of financial literacy, the demystification of complex wealth building strategies and the link to divine purpose for wealth in this book.

Placing Order for the Books

These books can be obtained from the following sources:

Haggai Business School

Email: HYPERLINK "mailto:haggaischool@yahoo.co.uk"
haggaischool@yahoo.co.uk
Tel: 234-1-8027782240

Online Orders

Amazon.com. You can also place online order via
HYPERLINK "mailto:imoabasi@yahoo.com" imoabasi@
yahoo.com